Unlocking Academic Achievement:

A Principal's Guide to Improved Measurable Results

by

David Young

Unlocking Academic Achievement: A Principal's Guide To Improved Measurable Results

Published by David Young
Danville, KY 40422
davidyo2024@gmail.com
www.davidyoungeducation.com

Edited by Mike Mavilia Rochester
Proofreader Michael Fedison
Layout by Sophie Hanks
Cover Design by Arash Jahani

ISBN (paperback): 979-8-9913875-0-7
ISBN (ebook): 979-8-9913875-1-4
Library of Congress Control Number: 2024922307

To Holly—Aside from being a wonderful wife and mom, thanks for being my thought partner in all things education. So much of what I've learned and the good things that have happened in my career have happened because of you.

And to Mason, Connor, and Emma—Thanks for enduring so many days and nights of "education talk" around the kitchen table and for always being my number one supporters. You three are the best things to ever happen to your mom and me.

Acknowledgments

Mike Lafavers - Superintendent (Boyle County Schools)
The strategies and systems that eventually became the core of *Measurable Results* began during the time that we were working together. Your motivational, accountability-driven, courageous, "what's best for kids" approach set a high level of expectation for student success and we worked hard every day to meet or exceed it. Thanks for being a great friend, colleague, and mentor.

Steve Burkich - Assistant Superintendent/Chief Academic Officer (Anderson County Schools) and Superintendent (Boyle County Schools)
As a new principal coming straight out of the classroom, I spent the first two years focused almost exclusively on instilling the best practices that I had seen you implement in our district. I witnessed the positive impact they had on the students in my

classroom, so I knew they were worth the work. Thank you so much for being a valuable mentor and friend.

Maureen Elwyn - Instructional Coach (Boyle County Schools)

You were the perfect partner as we implemented the core systems in all our schools. I've learned so much from you. I truly appreciate your friendship and support, as well as your feedback during the writing of *Measurable Results*.

Kevin Hub - Superintendent (Scott County Schools) and Executive In Residence (Eastern Kentucky University)

I can always count on you for honest opinions, feedback, and guidance. Thank you for helping me to create the absolute best version of everything I set out to do, and thanks especially for your feedback on *Measurable Results*.

Brian Buffington - Education Service Agency colleague (Pioneer RESA, Georgia) and National Consultant/Keynote Speaker

I truly value all of your support and feedback as we collaborate and challenge each other to improve. Thanks especially for your feedback on *Measurable Results*.

Amanda Burrows - Director of Academics (Central Kentucky Educational Cooperative)
The proofreading feedback you provided on *Measurable Results* made a huge difference! Thanks for taking the time to help me create the best possible version of this book.

Mike Rochester - *Measurable Results* **Lead Consultant**
From manuscript completion to publication, I have truly enjoyed the process. Thank you for your wisdom, feedback, and advice. It had a positive impact in the book, and it has also made me a better writer.

Rocky Wallace - Author, Professor (Campbellsville University)
Thank you for being such a wise and encouraging mentor for me in the past few years. You always bring me back to a focus on the heart of a servant leader. Thanks, as well, for your feedback during the writing of *Measurable Results*.

Kelly Middleton - Author, former Superintendent (Newport Independent Schools)
Thanks so much for taking the time to provide guidance to a new author like me and for making the introduction between Mike Rochester and me. Writing and publishing *Measurable Results* has been such a great experience. I appreciate your help!

TABLE OF CONTENTS

Introduction

I did not plan to become a principal. A teacher and coach? Yes, I knew I wanted to do those things since my early teens. I am competitive by nature, I like working in a team, and one day I realized that I loved helping others learn something new. It energized me, and after that, I never doubted that I wanted to teach and coach.

During my first few years teaching elementary school and coaching middle and high school boys' basketball, I started taking some master's degree classes toward principal certification. I didn't really think I wanted to be a principal, but at that time Kentucky required all teachers to get a master's degree. I thought, "*If I have to get a degree anyway, why not give myself some options late in my career when I'm old and ready to retire from coaching?*" That began my road to principal's certification. It was a backup degree that I assumed I would never use.

While taking those classes, though, I started to see connections between coaching and being a principal. As a coach, I loved inspiring my team. Principals certainly play a motivational role with their staff, teachers, and students. In coaching, I also enjoyed the process of scouting our next opponent and learning what they did well. This quality is important for principals, too. None of us are experts in everything, so we have to watch others and learn the effective strategies they use, and then try to incorporate those strategies into our schools. There were other parallels. Great coaches are great teachers, and coaching is an effective model for principals to use for teacher growth. In fact, strong principals put a great deal of effort into coaching teachers, helping them practice new strategies and improve their craft.

I mentioned that I am competitive, so giving my best in order to win is important. I found that being competitive helps when serving as a principal, as well. The wonderful thing about being a competitive principal, however, is that winning isn't about us—the adults in the school. Winning means children have learned more and have a better chance at a successful future. I will choose that type of winning over the outcome of a game any day. Once I started to recognize these parallels, my sights quickly became focused on becoming a principal.

I think the most important connection between coaching and being a principal might be the team mentality. As the leader of the school, my staff and students are all part of my team. Teamwork makes the challenge more fun, and let's face it, success is rarely achieved alone. Instead, it is a culmination of collaboration, connections with other talented colleagues, failures, lessons learned, and small steps forward. Over time, those small steps become pieces of a larger puzzle—a *system* that leads to success, built and implemented by you and your team.

As a principal, do not underestimate your role in the development and implementation of the systems that lead to success. You are the leader, the facilitator, the delegator, and the coach in the room. You must be reflective enough to process how the attempts become steps and how the steps become pieces of the larger puzzle. You may come up with some of the ideas that work, or you might help the group fail forward and learn a valuable lesson. Once you have been in leadership for a while, perhaps you will get to see something incredible happen as a direct result of the work that you and your team have done. That is what happened to me, and it is what led me to write *Unlocking Academic Achievement: A Principal's Guide to Improved Measurable Results*.

In two different schools where I served as principal, my leadership team and I made a commitment to learn from our most successful teachers, as well as from high-performing schools that we visited. We implemented what we learned, failed forward, and eventually created systems that led to success. In only a couple of years, those two schools improved from performing below the state average to performing in the top quarter of all schools in Kentucky.

Later in my career, I spent ten years at the district level as assistant superintendent – chief academic officer. My team and I implemented the systems from my prior schools in all of the schools in our district. We also learned, failed forward, expanded the systems, and created new elements that work in all grades K-12. Academic results improved drastically in every school. In each situation, the pathway to success was paved by our team. I can't adequately express what a valuable experience it was to implement systems that benefitted our students in such a visible way.

I am now chief executive officer at the Central Kentucky Educational Cooperative (CKEC). My staff and I work every day to train the schools and districts in our region to implement the core systems and best practices that my team and I honed during those years as assistant superintendent. We are driven by the idea that, in education, we are all in this together. When we learn something and verify that it works, is scalable, and has staying power, we should share it with each other. We should never waste an opportunity to help students experience greater success and to help our colleagues avoid the mistakes we made.

In this book, chapters one through six describe the foundational work that needs to be done by the principal to build a common language and instill some important mindsets within the school staff. Chapters seven through twelve incorporate those foundations and take you step-by-step through the two core systems that lead to significant improvement in academic success. My hope is that by sharing these Measurable Results systems with you, something amazing will happen for you, your staff, and your students.

1

Defining School Success Using Measurable Results

In my opinion, there is no more critical role in a school district than the principal. For a school to thrive, its principal must be adept at so many different roles. Head of safety and security, building-level CEO, delegator, mentor, coach, evaluator, counselor . . . the list goes on and on. Oh, and don't forget the most important role—we are in the business of educating kids, so the principal also has to be the instructional leader of the building. More on that in a minute, but we should quickly pause to acknowledge the stark reality of serving as the principal. It is a complex job, and it requires a skill set that very few possess. It is a position that should be held in high regard in our schools, districts, and communities.

Those of us who are (or have been) in the principal's role typically feel called to lead. It is in the fiber of our being to serve and to inspire others to do the same. We have a passion for helping children and their families. We realize that we can play a part in changing their life trajectory in a positive way—in the present and in the future. This is why we do it, and even when we have bad days, we wake up ready to do it again the next day. We are driven to make our students and schools successful.

Let's talk, then, about school success. How do we define it? Well, school success comes in many forms. First, there are subjective, or qualitative, measures of success. These are opinions, but they are worth our attention. How does the school feel? How does it seem like things are going? What do teachers, students, and parents say about the school? These questions and others like them can be answered by our stakeholders in anecdotes and stories they tell. We should listen closely and take these stories into consideration. But, when considering subjective data, it is important to focus on trends. Subjective measures of success should mostly be measured in bulk. Try to avoid getting caught up in each individual opinion or story.

Second, there are objective, or quantitative, measures of success. For our purposes, I'll call those *measurable results.* Like the subjective data, these measures do not tell the whole story, but they tell a large part of it. Instruments that produce quantitative, measurable results are not always perfect. It's true that they can be biased or have some small, design-oriented flaws. But this isn't typically the case, and it certainly isn't significant enough that we should discount the information we gather from them. Objective assessments produce concrete data that is generally not as easy to skew. The data simply says what it says—and it tells us something true.

When I was a basketball coach, a common saying among the players was, "The ball don't lie." In context, this meant that if the referee called a questionable foul on our team and the opposing player went to the line for a free throw (a free, uncontested shot), he would miss because he shouldn't have been shooting that free throw anyway. With measurable results, you could say something similar. The data is objective and difficult to skew. In other words, "the data don't lie." Whatever the measurable results say reflects something about the school and the performance of the students. If several data sources say similar things, then there is all the more reason to take them seriously.

Now, students are certainly more than a test score. There's no arguing that. Measurable academic results also aren't *everything*, but they are *something* . . . and something very important. These assessments are based on standards that students need to master. Inside those standards are important skills, content, and vocabulary that successful adults need to know and be able to utilize. When students achieve higher academic results, it is an indicator that they have mastered those standards at a higher level than before. That is extremely important. As a result, it is vital that teachers know how to effectively address standards through daily instruction, build units and lessons that are laser-focused, actively engage students, and accurately assess student mastery.

Before we move on, though, there is another important distinction between subjective and objective measures of success: people *hear* about the subjective measures, but they *see* the objective measures. Parents receive report cards, classroom test scores, benchmark assessments, state assessments, ACT/SAT results, Advanced Placement Scores and pass rates, and many others. The community, and sometimes the whole state, see these as well. Measurable results matter because they "don't lie," but also because they are visible to those outside your school and district.

In a school, a heavy focus on measurable results may seem daunting at first, but I have some good news. In academics, the fact that the results are measurable creates a valuable dynamic. As a principal pursuing improvement, you can collect measurable data and observe whether it improves in response to your adjustments. You can spend time in the classrooms where students produce the highest measurable results, learning what it is about the teacher's daily practice that leads to such success. Once you discover those practices, you can teach others to utilize those same practices in their classrooms, coaching and monitoring the results along the way. I'll talk about this in the next chapter. Finally, when measurable results improve, you and your staff will celebrate together. When the results don't improve, you will get into classrooms and work with your teachers to find out why and what is the best next step forward. This is a strong, healthy way to lead your school. Over time, operating this way will define your work as the instructional leader in the building.

You see, the principal's job is a hard one, with many facets. But here is a secret: all of the facets of the job are not equal. Some are more important than others, and some have more return on investment than others. Spend your time improving the measurable academic results of your students and you will see positive effects in many other areas. You will be in classrooms more, which means you will build better relationships with students. You will be out of your office in hallways, so the building will be safer. You will empower successful teachers and coach less successful teachers. When you talk with your staff, you will discuss the academic success and barriers facing individual students and the group as a whole. This will help you meet their needs. When a parent calls with concerns about a teacher, it will be easier to determine how likely it is that the parent's complaint is legitimate. Put simply, prioritize measurable academic success first. You will be a better leader, the students will perform at a higher level academically, and the school will become a better environment in which to learn.

In this book, we will take a deep dive into the mindsets and work that lead to significant improvement in measurable results. But for now, suffice it to say that measurable results are important. They impact our students, and they are worth the time you invest in them.

Questions for discussion:

1. *What made/makes you want to be a principal?*

   _____

   _____

   _____

2. *In your school or district, what kinds of qualitative and quantitative data are being gathered? How are they used?*

   _____

   _____

   _____

3. *What measurable result(s) would you like to see improved and why?*

   _____

   _____

   _____

2

Superstars

Early in my career as an elementary school teacher, my principal would regularly visit each classroom in the school. Her presence in my classroom made a huge impact on my performance and growth, as well as the performance of many of the teachers in our school. She unknowingly showed me how valuable it was for the principal to see instruction firsthand, rather sitting behind a desk in the office. When I became a principal myself, I carried her techniques with me. So, when I was looking for measurable results, I knew that there was only one place to get a preview of those results—the classroom. I spent copious amounts of time within the classrooms in my school and other schools I visited. Pretty soon, I came to an important conclusion. If I had to boil my job down to one sentence, it would be this: *In order to be successful as a principal, I must recognize who my superstar teachers are and make as many of my non-superstar teachers look, act, behave, and generally be like those superstars.* It really is that simple. Which teachers have the qualities of superstars? What teaching strategies make them so successful? And how can I scale those approaches and practices as widely as possible across my building?

I remember walking into classroom after classroom at Junction City Elementary School, the second school in which I served as principal. In the first few months, I dedicated a lot of time to identifying my superstar teachers. I had an idea of what I was looking for, but I needed to figure out how to convey this notion to others. So I began to formulate a list of what qualities superstar teachers had (see figure 1.1). I was fortunate to have at least one superstar in every grade level. My next task was to determine what teaching strategies these superstar teachers were using that were creating such positive measurable results.

Figure 1.1
What Are the Qualities of Superstar Teachers?

The most talented teachers in your building.	Get the best measurable results from the students.	Hold themselves to the highest standard.
Often work the hardest, but certainly the most efficiently.	Have great relationships with the students, and often inconvenience themselves for the students.	Exude the personality you want your building to have.

Once I identified the teachers who got the best measurable results, I spent time in those classrooms trying to learn what teaching strategies made them most successful. Specifically, I was looking for collaborative planning, spiral review, focus on standards, student engagement, transitions, and assessment. As I watched each of them, I began to see what the instruction looked like when the students performed at their highest level. My task quickly became organizing the elements in the most efficient way, which became the first steps toward creating a *system* for student success—and measurable results. My superstars all had their own unique talents and personalities, but I realized they also had many of the same common teaching strategies that were deeply rooted in daily instruction. These strategies were not talent-based. They were scalable, and this meant I could expand them to other classrooms and grade levels.

By the second semester, I started discussing these teaching strategies during my weekly professional learning community (PLC) meetings with each grade-level team. My superstars were invaluable in this process. Once I introduced a strategy, they would share how they used it in their lessons. These tips were affirming for my successful teachers and instructive for my teachers who needed improvement. In this small but important way, my superstar teachers began to have a school-wide impact. Right away, I began to see some success in scaling my superstar teachers' best practices into other classrooms.

A great influence on my development as a leader has been Todd Whitaker, author of many great books for teachers and principals including *What Great Teachers Do Differently* and *What Great Principals Do Differently*. In the latter, Todd spends a good deal of time talking about superstar teachers, even going as far as saying that we, as leaders, need to "cater to our superstars."[1] This doesn't mean that we need to form an "inner circle" of teacher confidants that is impenetrable to others within our staff. Instead, it means that in addition to hitting home runs in the classroom every day, our superstar teachers are also likely to see the bigger picture of school success—including structures and resources that contribute to the success. Principals need to remove all barriers that exist for these superstar teachers, clearing the way for them to be great. When they do great things, everyone can learn from them and principals can work to scale those best practices across the staff.

There are many added bonuses to identifying and leaning on your superstar teachers. I've found superstar teachers are innovative and willing to try new things responsibly. They can help you examine new approaches and decide whether they work in a responsible way, rather than "experimenting" with new ideas that could negatively impact students. Superstars can help principals decide when to move forward with something new, press *pause*, or move away from an idea altogether. They should be consulted (discreetly) as you make decisions that impact the school. If they say a decision or initiative is a good idea, it probably is. You should go for it, even if you are not getting the same glowing feedback from others in the staff. Conversely, if they say something is not a good idea or the timing isn't right, you should slow down or move completely away from the idea—even if you really want to make it happen. If your superstars are not on board, it is probably not going to be successful. You should move on to something else.

In every school in which I have worked, there has always been that one teacher who would discreetly pop into my office on a regular basis to help me keep my "finger on the pulse" of the school. Or to put it more plainly, to tell me what is (and isn't) going well. Now, let me be clear—I am not referring to a teacher who is being a gossip or a "tattler." Those often exist, as well, but I am referring to the teacher who truly wants the school to do well and realizes that I (the principal) need to be successful in order for that to occur. If this teacher is also a superstar, you should consider yourself very fortunate.

Once, I went to an out-of-district training session about connecting questions on unit assessments to specific learning targets and came back energized about what I learned. Spoiler alert, I'll talk more about these unit assessments and learning targets later on in the book. Implementing this concept was going to be a heavy lift for our school, but I thought it was definitely worth it. My leadership team was made up of my superstar teachers, so I scheduled a special leadership meeting for later in the week. When the day came, I could not wait to share it with the group. I was convinced that they would be as excited as I was. Once the meeting started, I began telling them about what I had learned. They were polite, of course, and you could even tell that they thought it was a pretty good idea. But there was hesitation, and I could feel it. Near the end of the meeting, one of the teachers spoke up and said, "Would it be okay if we think about it and get together again next week to talk about it some more?" I said of course, and we ended the meeting.

The next day, one of the teachers on the leadership team stopped in to see me. She said, "Hey, I just wanted to let you know that the idea you shared with us yesterday is a good one. I think we all see that it could really help us and our students." Then she chuckled and said, "But if we try to implement it right now, I think the school is going to explode. We love the things that we are doing to improve, but change is stressful. If we could wait just a little bit, I think it would give the staff time to implement the new things and then be ready to do what we discussed yesterday."

If this had been a teacher who was not a hard worker, a student-focused professional, or simply wasn't a superstar, I might have kept on going with the plan. But that was not the case. This teacher was one of my hardest-working, most conscientious, and talented teachers. Her students always excelled, and she was willing to go to great lengths to make sure they had every barrier removed. If she said the timing was bad, I believed it. So, I paused. I met with my leadership team and asked if they thought we should just slow down a little and let the staff have time to acclimate to the changes already in progress. They answered with a resounding "Yes!" We waited a few months, laid the foundation for the new work in the late spring, and did the work that following summer. It became a game changer for our school. But if I had not listened to my superstar teachers, it would have been met with major resistance and would have likely failed forever.

Making changes that lead to measurable results in academics is going to take some work, and you need your superstars on board. If you can pull together a leadership team made up of your superstars, it is highly recommended. Spend time learning together about the concepts that come later in this book, as well as discussing the right timing and implementation plan. Allow them to begin some of the work in their own classrooms so that they can play a role when it is time to train other staff members. If you cannot pull together a team of superstars, you will still need to consult with them informally. Stop in during their planning times, before school, or after school to chat. Be sure, however, to also stop in all teachers' classrooms for conversations—again, you do not want your superstars viewed as the "inner circle" or some type of exclusive club. All teachers need time for conversation with you, but like students in our classrooms, those conversations need to be differentiated. You won't talk about the same things with your superstar teachers as your non-superstar teachers. I highly recommend differentiating teachers by levels. It may feel harsh or judgmental, but I've found it is an important way to know what each teacher needs and how you can help them. As you begin this journey, laying the foundation is essential—and that begins with your superstars.

Questions for discussion:

1. Looking at the six qualities of identifying a superstar, which of your teachers come to mind? Are there some who possess nearly all of those qualities? If so, where do they need a little support to help them grow?

   _____

   _____

   _____

2. Consider the principal's role boiled down to one sentence: **In order to be successful as a principal, I must recognize who my superstar teachers are and make as many of my non-superstar teachers look, act, behave, and generally be like those superstars.** How do you anticipate that the climate and culture of your school will begin to change when you start making progress toward this goal?

   _____

   _____

   _____

3. Have you ever "pressed pause" in response to a request from a superstar teacher? What was the result?

   _____

   _____

   _____

4. *Think about creating a leadership team of your superstars. How will you navigate the formation of the team without creating the perception of an "inner circle of favorites"?*

_____

_____

_____

3

We Control Our Destiny

With your superstars identified and mobilized, you are ready to start working with your staff to instill some of the mindsets that are common in high-performing schools. One such mindset pertains to the idea of destiny. Improving measurable academic results is hard work, and it is common for teachers to contemplate whether improvement is even a possibility. Consciously or subconsciously, they may ask questions like, "Are the barriers we face too great?" "Where and how do we begin the improvement process?" "Whose expertise should we seek?" and "Who ultimately controls our ability to achieve our goals?"

As I mentioned in the Introduction, I was assistant superintendent—chief academic officer in a district in central Kentucky for ten years before I began my current job as CEO at CKEC. Before that, I was an elementary school principal. In both of those roles, I was very interested in what made great teachers and schools perform at high levels. I spent lots of time in all of the high-performing classrooms in my school, and I also made time to visit dozens of high-performing schools during those years. As I visited classrooms, traveled to other schools, and communicated with colleagues in other schools and districts, I began to see something interesting about the outlook these successful professionals had.

In schools with average measurable results, I noticed that the staff and leadership badly wanted to improve their performance and were even successful in identifying the correct growth areas, but they always felt that they had to find an expert practitioner from outside the district to teach them how to improve. I think we have all been in those professional learning sessions, listening to someone we have never met teach us what we are doing wrong and how to do better. There is nothing innately wrong with outside expertise. Sometimes you need someone from the outside teaching you how you might change your practices in order to help students achieve higher results. Or you may need an outside practitioner to build background knowledge, kick off the work with your leadership team, and then step aside as the work begins. These are certainly acceptable uses of outside expertise.

However, many of the high-performing schools I visited had a different mentality. They operated on the premise that there were professionals on staff in the school, at the district level, or in another school within the district who had the expertise needed for the school to improve in a specific growth area. If this expertise didn't exist, the school believed that the staff contained professionals who were talented, bright, and dynamic and could develop the needed expertise in a short time frame through research, spending time with an outside expert, and/or participating in pilot work. In these schools, the in-house experts trained their colleagues, and this approach contributed to their high-level measurable results.

In my early days as chief academic officer, one of my schools' major growth areas was writing. We simply weren't giving students enough opportunities to write, and the support to become proficient writers. Specifically, we noted there was an imbalance in the time teachers spent working on published pieces versus practicing on-demand writing. We made a conscious effort to improve, but we soon realized that we were implementing versions of the strategies we'd always used. They still weren't working, but we couldn't figure out what we should do differently. Over the course of a couple of years, we brought in some writing experts from outside the school who knew the recipe for success. These training opportunities seemed good, but what we learned from them never seemed to have staying power in our schools.

Finally, we had the realization that a writing expert actually worked on our staff. Maureen was a former middle school English / language arts teacher who had transitioned to an instructional coach at one of our elementary schools. Even without elementary or high school classroom teaching experience, a few things led us to think of Maureen. First, she was known as a great middle school writing teacher when she was in the classroom. Second, her elementary school had become a high performer since she became the instructional coach there. And third, she was an integral part of our Measurable Results implementation districtwide, so she understood the nuances of our best practices.

We talked to Maureen and asked if she would help us improve writing instruction across the entire district. She accepted, and over the course of a few days the following summer, she delivered professional learning for all teachers and administrators. The difference was immediately evident. Maureen is a superstar teacher and coach, so her content was fantastic. That was no surprise. But the fact that the teachers were receiving training from a colleague they knew and trusted changed the atmosphere in the room.

Maureen was instrumental in helping our English teachers redesign their lesson structures, bank writing prompts to use daily with students, and collaboratively meet in teams to analyze student writing pieces. She also helped teachers find a balance between writing for publication and on-demand writing opportunities. After receiving Maureen's training, classroom implementation happened at a different level than ever before. You could almost feel the teachers thinking, *This will definitely work because Maureen says it does.* When teachers had questions during the year, Maureen was only an email or phone call away. Did it impact student achievement? You bet it did. Within just a couple of years, writing improved in all schools and became an area of strength in our district.

When a staff believes that the expertise needed for improvement lies within, it opens up a world of possibilities and ancillary benefits. It empowers your superstar teachers, developing their abilities as coaches and leaders. It also provides authenticity to your professional learning opportunities for teachers. Professional learning feels different when a teacher's growth areas are being supported by a colleague, and in most cases, someone he or she respects.

As the principal, you are not required to have all the answers. But it is important that you are able to find them and recognize them when you see them. Professional learning provided in-house sets the principal up to play this role. Tapping into expertise that lies within your school will propel the school forward academically. This is huge for you as an instructional leader. It communicates the message that "we are in control of our own destiny." Although there is a time and place in which outside expertise makes sense, a powerful shift occurs when an entire staff believes that everything needed to ensure that students perform at high academic levels resides within its own hallways, workspaces, and classrooms. Principals of high-performing schools craft this narrative: "Our school has everything it needs right here, within our school/district." Your words matter, and your actions speak volumes about what it takes for the school to achieve its goals. As often as possible, focus your improvement efforts within the expertise that exists inside the staff.

Questions for discussion:

1. What expertise already exists among teachers in your building? Are you maximizing it? If not, where can you start?

   _____

   _____

   _____

2. What expertise is needed in your building? Is someone on staff capable of learning and developing in this area?

   _____

   _____

   _____

3. Do your teachers believe that the school controls its own destiny? If not, what do they believe are the obstacles that stand in the way of success?

   _____

   _____

   _____

4

Congruence

It is fascinating how mindsets can sometimes be as powerful as practices. They color how we view our work. In addition to "we control our destiny," let's talk about one more important mindset: congruence. It's really a simple concept. Lessons, units, and classroom assessments need to be driven by standards. Once in place, everything in the lesson or unit—including teaching resources and questions asked—needs to be *perfectly* aligned to the verb, key nouns, and context within the standard. That's congruence. When it comes to improved measurable results in academics, I believe developing a congruence mindset is the top priority that schools should have. Nothing else is close.

When I train teachers and principals on congruence, I often use a metaphor involving the invisible gas called radon. Several years ago, there were a variety of public service announcements that went out on television and radio about the dangers of radon. If you are not familiar, radon quietly seeps out of the ground in some areas and into houses or workplaces. It has no smell, and with prolonged exposure, it causes cancer. You need to have a radon detector in order to realize it is there. Because it is invisible and odorless, the public service announcements called radon "the silent killer." Like radon, you won't notice congruence unless you know what you are looking for and how to look for it.

In 2018, a comprehensive report was released by The New Teacher Project.[2] The report, called *The Opportunity Myth*, was based on an extensive study that had been done in classrooms across several school districts. All types of schools were included:

- elementary, middle, and high
- urban, suburban, and rural
- high poverty, affluent, and middle class
- district and charter
- high, medium, and low minority rates
- high, medium, and low rates of students identified with disabilities

In the study, researchers observed nearly one thousand lessons looking for only two things:

1. What standard is the teacher intending to teach today?
2. How well does that standard align with the work the students are being asked to complete?

In other words, the study was looking for congruence. Unfortunately, they found that classrooms in schools with high populations of minority students, students who live in poverty, or students with disabilities had poor alignment between the standard the teacher intended to teach and the work the students were doing. What is even more concerning, however, is that a lack of congruence was prevalent across classrooms with *all* types of student populations. This has broad implications for all of us as educational leaders.

The findings of *The Opportunity Myth* match up with what I see as I have visited schools throughout my career, even to this day. It is not true in every classroom, of course, and it is not an indictment on the ineptitude of teachers. Often, the congruence mindset is simply missing. Once instilled, congruence is a game changer. But like the radon comparison I made earlier, it is easy to miss if you don't know what you are looking for.

When I was a classroom teacher, I had never heard of the term *congruence*, and we did not talk about alignment with standards much, either. There were no such things as learning targets created from the standards, and we certainly did not talk about the verb, key nouns, and context within the standards. You know what we did? I was given a textbook, and I was asked to teach from it. We focused a lot on the importance of using key vocabulary, but there was little discussion about standards. Congruence is predicated on lessons driven by standards. We were textbook or program-driven, so we just didn't think about it—at least not in the laser-focused way that high performance requires

Back in those days, my principal (who was fabulous and great about doing walk-through observations) would pop in to my classroom and watch me teach. I might have been delivering what appeared to be a great lesson—actively engaging the students, using key vocabulary, asking rigorous verbal and written formative assessment questions, providing hands-on materials, and so on. To the untrained eye, I was excelling. But in hindsight, I can admit that I was not making sure that I assessed according to the verb in the grade-level standard. The verb in the standard might have been "justify where a mathematical rule comes from," but in my seemingly stellar lesson, I wasn't ever actually requiring the students to justify their answers or reasoning. I might have had them explain or describe the mathematical rule, but not justify it. Looking back, I think I probably did this often. I felt like I was excelling nearly every day, and I was getting great feedback from parents and my administrators. But when we got to the end of the year and students took the state assessment, they never performed at a level that seemed commensurate with the quality of instruction happening daily in my classroom. They underperformed, and none of us could figure out why. I recognize now that it was a lack of congruence between the state standards that should have been driving my lesson, the verbal and written questions I was using as formative assessment, and the resources I was using to teach. I was not teaching in a way that was congruent to the standards. As a result, my students underperformed on the state assessment—which was built to reflect those same standards. It should not have been a shock to us. It is a fairly simple concept, but it takes intentional planning to implement. It is easy to assume that fun, engaging, active lessons are congruent with standards. Sometimes, they aren't. It's up to us to make sure they are.

After I was introduced to the concept of congruence as a principal, it quickly became a lens through which I viewed instruction in my building. Not surprisingly, I saw many teachers—even superstar teachers—doing exactly what I had done. They were working hard and teaching lessons that were otherwise very good. But they were not congruent.

You will see congruence woven throughout this guide to school success. For high-level academic results, teachers and administrators must recognize that congruence extends in an unbroken line from the standard, to the learning targets, to the resources being used to teach, to the formative assessment questions at the end of a lesson and unit of study. It is the common thread that weaves the Measurable Results system together, and I cannot overstate its importance. If I became a principal again today, a congruence awareness and mindset is the first thing I would instill in my staff.

Consider this: If teachers fail to teach and assess congruently for a day, it is probably not a huge problem. But if they make this mistake every day, or the majority of days, for a semester . . . a year . . . multiple years? Even if other best practices are in place students in these classrooms are not receiving on-grade-level instruction. Just like the example from my own classroom, students in these classes will underperform on state or national assessments and no one will be able to figure out why.

Questions for discussion:

1. Can you think of examples of assignments or lessons in your own classroom or school that lacked congruence?

   _____

   _____

   _____

2. What are some indicators of congruence that you might look for when you enter a classroom to observe?

   _____

   _____

   _____

3. In an effort to encourage a congruence mindset among your teachers, how might you address it in a professional learning community (PLC)?

   _____

   _____

   _____

5

Guarantees

As we navigate our daily lives, have you ever noticed the extent to which we depend on certain unspoken guarantees? For instance, when I go to the supermarket, I operate with the assumption that the food will be of good quality and not spoiled. I just pick out the foods I want and buy them. These unspoken guarantees are a luxury we have that do not exist in many areas of the world. I cannot remember the last time I bought something at the supermarket that was significantly expired or not edible due to spoilage. It rarely happens, and it is an incredible guarantee that is an integral part of my life.

Here is another example: I recently bought a used vehicle. It was 4 years old with 32,000 miles on it. The dealership told me that they did a thorough mechanical diagnostic overview and tune-up of the vehicle, and it was in perfect condition. We all have heard horror stories of someone buying a "lemon" vehicle, but thousands of cars are bought every day with the assurance of such a guarantee. I bought that vehicle, and I fully believe that with the proper upkeep, I will be able to drive it with no major problems for 150,000 to 200,000 miles. So far, so good. It now has over 80,000 miles on it, and I have had no problems with it. What a blessing to have guarantees like these!

There are other great examples that come to mind. I keep my money in the bank. I never seriously consider the possibility that the money will not be there when I attempt to use it. It is an unspoken guarantee that has a huge impact on my life. When I order or send a package, it is a guarantee that it will eventually arrive at its destination. When I turn on the light switches in my house or plug a device into an electrical outlet, I operate based on the guarantee that the power I need will be there. The list goes on and on.

From a business standpoint, why are guarantees like these important? It starts with the critical tenets of consistency and quality. If a business can provide a good or service that is consistently of such high quality that I do not even have to think about it, I am likely to become a repeat customer. Not only that, but I am going to tell my friends about the quality of the product or service. This is good for the business financially, and it is good for me, too, because I am consistently having a positive experience. When this happens over the course of time, it produces one of the most powerful feelings that humans experience. It produces *trust*.

Once I trust that something in my life is going to happen consistently—at a high quality and without me even thinking about it—my relationship with this good or service enters a different realm. It is now a win-win for all involved. The company has my repeat business, so they win. I have less stress in my life, so I win. I trust that they are going to do what they always do and do it well, so I just enjoy the fruits of that guarantee. I can live my life and use my brainpower to focus on other, less guaranteed efforts.

In our schools, parents and students are looking for similar guarantees. Safety and student well-being are a given. Parents must feel safe sending their children to school every day, and most schools have embraced the need for this guarantee. Even with the increased violence that we hear about in schools these days, safety and student well-being are a high priority in many schools. They are working to make sure that this guarantee is felt by their students and families.

Our students and parents deserve the same guarantee of consistency and high quality in measurable academic results. In the coming chapters, we are going to get into step-by-step directions for utilizing and maximizing our system that leads to improved student achievement. The work begins with the acknowledgment that schools need academic guarantees in the areas of standards, curriculum, instruction, and assessment.

This is where the mindsets and approaches outlined in this book begin to converge. Earlier, we discussed the importance of your superstar teachers and the critical staff mindsets around congruence and "we control our destiny." As you begin the journey toward academic guarantees, these mindsets are critical, and your superstars will play a pivotal role.

From a parent's perspective, one might ask academic questions such as:

- If my child goes to your school, what will the teachers consistently teach on a daily basis? Is it the state standards or a program the school bought?
- If my child struggles today, how will the teacher know it? Is there a way that teachers monitor each child's mastery of lesson content every day? Will I know it so that I can help him/her?

Is there a guaranteed time for reteaching if my child is struggling?

- In lessons across all classrooms in the school, what is the primary mode of teaching? Is it lecture-based? Small-group oriented? What type of learning experiences can I expect for my child?
- How often in daily lessons are students actively engaged in learning, as opposed to being passively engaged and simply listening?

If you and your staff can address questions like these with some guarantees, you can begin the journey toward quality and consistency. Once students—and by extension, their parents—routinely experience these guarantees in every classroom, you will see multiple benefits.

In one of my schools, the leadership team and I decided to come up with a slogan to define who we were as a school. We landed on "Whatever It Takes." Our leadership team loved it. We all believe that we will do whatever it takes for students to be successful, so we adopted the slogan. We ordered a gigantic banner to hang outside our front door so that students and parents would see it each day. We also committed to letting it guide our decision-making. Whenever we were faced with a tough decision that presented a significant barrier, we would ask ourselves, "What does 'Whatever It Takes' mean in this situation?" The answer had to be within reason, of course, but we were willing to go to great lengths to ensure that our students were successful.

Interestingly, a few parents questioned the slogan. They would say, "Listen, we love the school and we think you guys are great. But when you say 'Whatever It Takes,' what does that mean? And how is it different from what you're doing now?" This was good for us because it made us confront those key questions as a staff. I relayed our discussions to those parents, and teachers began talking to parents, as well.

A big turning point occurred when we developed our guarantees and started sharing those. Statements like "Our daily lessons will be driven by learning targets from the Kentucky standards," "We will regularly use student data to make instructional decisions," and "We will provide daily intervention and reteaching when students struggle to learn the content" communicated, in a clear and concise way, our promises to the children who attended our school. Our guarantees added much-needed detail to "Whatever It Takes" in the areas of standards, curriculum, instruction, and assessment. In this way, the unspoken guarantees of our motto transitioned into a set of concrete promises. Parents appreciated these details. It solidified our resolve to meet the academic needs of students as a school and galvanized the efforts of our staff.

As administrators, we do not want every teacher to be an exact replica of the next one. However, there are core elements that should be in place in all classrooms. When guarantees are in place, the staff will begin to speak the same language and work on similar skills and practices. This streamlines improvement efforts. Once the guarantees take hold, parents will start to experience that powerful feeling we mentioned before— *trust*. When trust is instilled, parental support follows. At this point, you begin building a foundational culture of excellence that is recognized and experienced by students, parents, and staff. It's a win, win, win . . . and positive momentum will start building in your school.

Questions for discussion:

1. How do you think a set of academic guarantees might affect the perception of your school to staff, students, and parents?

    _____

    _____

    _____

2. Can you think of a school-related or non-school-related example of a time when a guarantee led you to develop a level of trust in a person or organization?

    _____

    _____

    _____

3. What specific guarantee questions can you think of that parents may have about your school?

    _____

    _____

    _____

6

Learning Targets

One last topic before getting into the Measurable Results system is an element that connects the system: learning targets. Learning targets are the driver of each day's lesson. They must be pulled directly from the grade-level standard, congruent to the standard, and bite-sized—which means they can be taught and assessed in one lesson.

For instance, take a standard like "Use addition and subtraction within twenty to solve word problems using situations of adding to, taking from, putting together, taking apart, and comparing, with unknowns in all positions." There's a lot to process and a lot to teach in that standard. It would be virtually impossible to teach all of that in one lesson, so a congruent, bite-sized learning target from that standard might be, "I can use subtraction within twenty to solve word problems involving taking apart and comparing." It's focused and achievable, for both the students and the teacher.

Once learning targets for the year are comprehensively written from the standards, congruence throughout each day's lesson is imperative. Creating bite-sized learning targets directly from the standard and teaching them with a laser focus makes a huge difference in the quality of lessons, as well as the learning experienced by the student. In many ways, learning targets are the linchpin of the Measurable Results system.

As a classroom teacher, I remember a few times when "magic" happened. I'd be teaching a particular concept, and the class just did not understand what I was trying to convey. I would try saying it a different way, showing a new technique, exploring it from a different perspective, using examples . . . you name it. I just could not break through. Then, suddenly, I said or demonstrated the right thing. Immediately, the class got it. I could almost see the "light bulbs" come on over their little heads. The energy in the room became supercharged and positive. It was a beautiful experience. At that moment, I would say to myself, "*This* is why I became a teacher. I'm watching students' understanding of the world—and their likelihood of success in life—broaden before my eyes. I have realized the potential impact that I have as an educator, and to be honest, I think I'm pretty awesome at my job!"

As teachers, we live for those "Aha!" moments in our students. It reminds us why we got into education in the first place, and that rush of dopamine that we get makes us feel productive and successful. You can tell I am heading for a "*Yeah, but . . .*," right?

The problem is, while those moments are golden, they can also be addictive. Pretty soon, you may subconsciously structure your lessons so that the students can't tell where the lesson is going. You teach, teach, teach, and then suddenly reveal the concept, skill, or content for the day. In your mind, the element of surprise makes the learning engaging for all. And, most importantly, you may get to see those "light bulbs" come on again—affirming your choice of profession and proving that you can make a difference in the world.

Don't let me be a wet blanket here—you *did* choose a fantastic profession and you *can* make a huge difference in the world. But, while the "light bulb" model can be affective at times, it should not be your go-to lesson structure most days. A lesson structure that revolves around a congruent learning target communicates clearly to students what the intended learning is for each day and gives them context for their experiences during the lesson. The lesson can still be dynamic and engaging without relying on the element of surprise. I'll discuss lesson structure in much more detail in a future chapter. For now, just remember that lessons driven by a clearly articulated learning target or targets are much more effective than those designed for "Aha!" moments.

I mentioned earlier that when I was a teacher and even early in my career as a principal, we didn't spend much time on standards. So, learning targets from standards definitely were not something I had heard about. I can remember the first time I saw them. I was visiting a high-performing school and walked into a classroom. On the board was a simple sentence that began with "I *can* . . ." It said something like, "I *can solve multiplication problems.*" As I talked with the teacher later, she explained that the learning targets she used were statements that she made up while planning. She simply wanted to state for the students what they would be learning and/or doing that day. She shared that she was pleased that, after only a week or so of using these statements, she began to see students looking at the board first thing in the morning or at the beginning of a lesson to see what they would be learning that day.

She had also seen an increase in measurable academic results. This teacher had discovered something important about teaching. Surprise can be a powerful tool, for sure. It is fun and engaging, but it has to be used in very small doses. I would say that it is best if it is always unplanned and spontaneous. The teacher, as well are her colleagues in this high-performing school, had learned that the best way to teach is to become laser-focused on the bite-sized chunk of learning for the day and tell the students what they are about to learn.

If you think about it, we all have the desire to know what is coming next. When we do, it allows us to give context to the new information or skill by connecting to previous knowledge and accessing prior experiences. While some of us like to be surprised or to have our eyes suddenly opened to a new concept, it is not a consistently effective approach to instruction. It is far better to let the students in on the secret before learning begins. Learning targets do just that.

Since those days, I have come a long way toward understanding the most effective models for developing and utilizing learning targets. Most importantly, I have learned how to derive the targets directly from the grade-level standards. As described in the previous story, this will lead to increased student interest in each day's lesson as well as improved grades and test scores.

The most important function of learning targets, however, is that they are the starting point for congruence and the cornerstone of the Measurable Results system. Without learning targets that are congruent to the grade-level standards, the system won't flourish. Sadly, the student impact will be diminished. The importance of quality learning targets cannot be understated.

Think about it this way: If the Measurable Results system was a large door that opened our schools, classrooms, and students to a world of academic success, learning targets would be the hinges of the door. All of the other parts *swing* from the learning target *hinge*. When the hinge is strong and of good quality, the door swings efficiently. Once the learning target is written congruently to the standard, everything in the lesson is driven by the target and must be congruent to it— the resources used, the questions asked (written and verbal), and assessments at the end of the lesson or unit. Conversely, if the learning targets are not well-written and perfectly congruent, it really does not matter how good the rest of the lesson or unit is. It simply will not produce the high levels of standards mastery and academic results that you desire.

Learning targets allow teachers to create more focused, intentional unit plans. As mentioned before, state standards can be extremely overwhelming. Many have so much content and skill packed in them that even if you can decipher everything that needs to be learned, there is little chance that you can teach a lesson (or sometimes even a short series of lessons) that adequately addresses the entirety of the standard. From a teacher's perspective, teaching all of the standards might feel like throwing a dart at a gigantic map each day and hoping to hit all the right destinations by the end of the year. Learning targets organized into units make unit planning, like lesson planning, more purposeful, focused, and efficient. This creates a whole new dynamic for a teacher. I am no longer throwing a dart at a gigantic map. Now I am shooting an arrow at a bull's-eye.

For lesson planning driven by learning targets, teachers should adhere to the daily guidelines below. Improved measurable academic results will follow:

1. Start the lesson with a quality target or two that is congruent to grade-level standards.
2. End the lesson with questions that are perfectly congruent to the target.
3. Actively engage students multiple times during the lesson.
4. Only use congruent resources and verbal questions (including programs) during the lesson.

There are nuances and special circumstances in every classroom and in every school. But simply considering what you now know about congruence, superstars, guarantees, and learning targets, you already have enough to impact the standards mastery level for many, many students. Improved standards mastery leads to an increase in measurable academic results.

Questions for discussion:

1. As educators, most of us have experienced "light bulb" moments in our classrooms. Can you think of a time that this happened in your classroom? What is the hidden danger?

   _____

   _____

   _____

2. Have you ever seen or used learning targets in the classroom? If so, how were they used and what effects did you notice?

   _____

   _____

   _____

3. In your own words, how could using learning targets to drive daily instruction lead to improved measurable results?

   _____

   _____

   _____

7

The Trunk of the Tree

In my backyard, I have several white pine trees that are very large. I don't know how much you know about white pines, but I have learned that they grow very quickly. They can mature from saplings to sizable trees in only a few years, which is why many local and regional conservation offices give out free white pine saplings on Arbor Day. They also provide great shade for your yard and are a welcome habitat for several beautiful species of birds, such as redbirds, bluebirds, finches, and other species. They are hearty trees with several positive characteristics.

As you can imagine, though, there are negatives. White pines can be fragile and even dangerous. They become huge in about ten to fifteen years, and the parts we see above ground grow much more quickly than the root system. The branches and needles are dense, so white pines catch big gusts of wind easily and can topple over. But that's not all; there is something else that can make them dangerous. White pines are a type of softwood, which means they are really susceptible to termites and other insects that love to burrow into their trunk and eat away at the wood. Every year or so, I notice that one of my trees has some sawdust-looking debris at the bottom of the trunk. With a little closer inspection, I can usually see some insects working into the trunk and slowly eating away at the tree's livelihood. Between this and the weak root system, I have to be careful with the tree because I know it is only a matter of time before it comes down. I have been through the process of removing a few of my white pines already, so I have become keenly observant of their health.

When we first moved into our house, one of the largest white pines was located right out our back door beside a wide, flat space we called "the ball field." My children (triplets) used to play every type of "ball" known to man in that space—kickball, softball, baseball, football . . . you name it, they played it. The tree often served as first base, a place to hide during hide-and-seek, and a safe space during games of tag.

One day, I was out in the "ball field" and noticed that some of the branches of the tree were not the same shade of green as the others. They were a lighter, pale green. It was interesting, but I did not think too much of it. I just made a mental note and moved on. But I kept watching—each day when we came out, other branches began turning a paler green. The original branches I noticed were starting to turn brown. As I inspected the tree, I made my first discovery of the declining health of the trunk due to insect damage.

I hated it, and the kids did, too. We loved that tree, and it was an integral part of the "ball field." We wanted to save it, but once the trunk was unhealthy, the branches did not stand a chance. It is a downer of a story, but the tree declined pretty rapidly, soon became a safety hazard, and we had to remove it.

> *Without a healthy trunk, a tree can't thrive—no matter how much attention you give the rest of the tree.*

There is a comparison here to be drawn to the academic endeavors in our schools. As principals, many of the issues we spend our time on are "in the branches" (see figure 1.2). We try to improve academic results by taking on initiatives like selecting a stellar math program, increasing student engagement, creating structures for Multi-Tiered Systems of Support (MTSS), selecting powerful tech devices and software, or a variety of other well-intentioned efforts. Our heart is in the right place. Those things really *do* need attention and improvement, and they really *can* improve measurable results.

Figure 1.2
The Trunk of the Tree for School Success

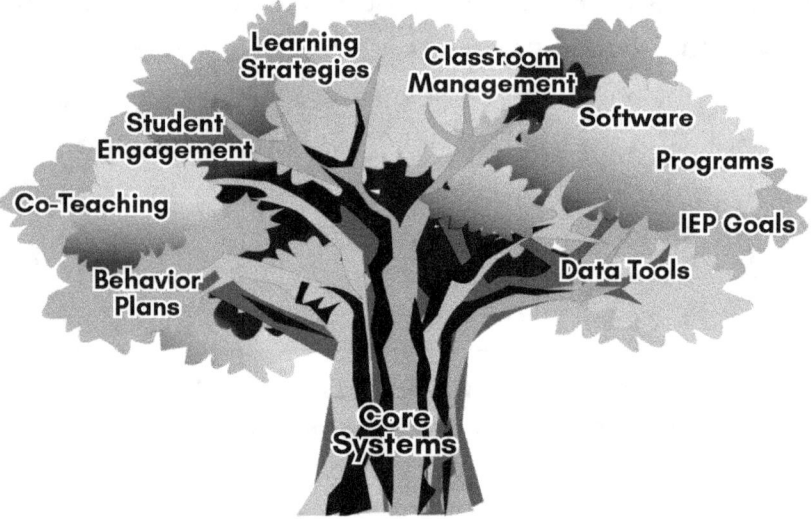

However, if we have not done the work to create core systems for unit and daily lesson design, the work on those issues that are "in the branches" just will not take hold. These core systems make up the "trunk of the tree" that lead to improved measurable results. If work "in the branches" is not connected to a solid, healthy tree trunk, it will turn to a paler shade of green, then brown, and eventually die—no matter how much attention, time, and effort we give it. Like many initiatives, we will feel like we invested an incredible amount of time, funding, and energy into "the branches," only to realize that our work had very little impact. A few years later, we will find ourselves back at square one, frustrated and working on the same issues. It is an exhausting cycle.

Let's consider the following scenario that you may have encountered. A teacher is hired as the new principal of ABC Elementary. She begins work on July 1, and she immediately begins to research the school to make sure she knows the school's strengths and areas for growth before the school year begins. She looks at all of the information that is readily available, including state accountability results and interim benchmark results in reading and math from the previous two years. She notices that the results for reading are pretty strong, but the math results are significantly lower. She concludes that she needs to find out more about math. What is the school doing when it comes to math standards, assessment, resources, software, and pedagogy? Have the teachers received quality training in math instruction? Are there other sources of math data that might provide more perspective?

As the principal is investigating over the next few weeks, teachers start to stop by and introduce themselves. They are beginning to trickle in to work in their classrooms and prepare for the school year. As the principal gets to know them, she decides to get their feedback on the low math results. "I notice that we are pretty strong in reading," she says. "I am very excited about that, and I think it says a lot about our potential for success across the board. If we can harness the abilities we have shown in reading and extend those to other subjects, the sky's the limit for us. However, I see that we aren't achieving at a very high level in math. What are your thoughts on why we might be underachieving in math?"

The teachers ponder the question and then begin to share their thoughts. One might say, "Well, we did some training in math last year. It was pretty good, but I think we could use some more. We have many hands-on math resources. We could always use more, but we are in pretty good shape as far as math materials. One big problem, though, is the quality of our math program. It is simply awful. I can tell you that I, for one, did not want to purchase that program when we decided to a few years ago. It is a major problem, and I would say it is affecting our students' ability to show academic success in math." Other teachers join in, expressing their disdain for the program, and the principal takes this feedback to heart. She says to herself, "I think that must be the problem. We need to purchase a new math program."

The principal begins the long, arduous process of preparing for the purchase of a new math program. She does everything exactly right. She appoints a group of teachers to explore the math programs other schools are using and the group reaches out to the schools to talk with them about their experiences with their program. The group narrows the choices down to three programs. Next, the principal calls together a larger group of teachers, parents, a board member, and a student. She tasks them with analyzing each program for standards alignment, scope and sequence, rigorous questions, real-life connections, and quality resources. The group even uses a program analysis and comparison worksheet provided by the state department of education.

Eventually, the group narrows it down to their number one choice. They do a presentation with the faculty and set aside a couple of weeks for all teachers to review samples from the top three programs, review the comparison worksheet findings from the group, and give final feedback to the group. After this period of time, the feedback is considered and a final choice is made. The program is purchased for $87,000.

Now, it is time for implementation to begin. In the summer, the school sets aside two professional development days for staff to be trained on the new program. This eliminates training in a couple of other high-need areas, but math is a priority and the training is highly recommended by the company that created the program. It is part of the purchased package. The teachers complete the training, prep for implementation, and begin the next school year using the program as the driving force behind future student success in math.

In December of year one, the school gives its normal mid-year benchmark assessment. The principal sees some improvement in measurable math results, but truthfully, it is not nearly as much improvement as she was hoping to see. She decides that it is still early, though, and she needs to get into classrooms more to see the program's implementation in action.

At the end of year one, the school measures again—this time with both the district-purchased benchmark assessment and the statewide math assessment. Once again, the principal sees a small amount of improvement, but it is still underwhelming. As she looks to the summer and the beginning of year two, the principal begins to have some doubts. She wonders if the teachers are implementing the program with fidelity. She decides that she will use the summer to provide more training to all staff, while also purchasing some additional resources and materials. Lack of resources and training must be the problem. Summer training comes and goes, and the next school year begins with a bang. Teachers are determined that year two will be the year when measurable results in math begin to show.

Winter break comes, and along with it, mid-year benchmark results in math. Frustratingly, the principal is again underwhelmed as she sees that math results have improved ever so slightly, but not significantly. She becomes convinced that while the teachers are telling her that they are implementing the program with fidelity, using the resources she purchased, and applying the training they received, they are not doing so in reality. She starts to become doubtful and short-tempered when discussing it with teachers, and they notice. She doubles down on walk-through observations during math lessons, but the visits now seem negative and punitive. Not surprisingly, at the end of year two, the school has shown little additional improvement in math results. During years three and four, the teachers begin to drift away from the new math program. Math becomes a sore spot for conversation when it comes up.

At the end of year four, the principal leaves ABC Elementary for a position in a new district. A new principal is hired in the school. He begins work on July 1 and immediately begins to research the school to make sure he knows strengths and areas for growth before the school year begins. He notices that the measurable results in reading are pretty strong, but the math results are significantly lower. He concludes that he needs to find out more about math. As the principal gets to know his teachers, he decides to get their feedback on the low math results. The teachers say, "Well, we did some math training in the past few years. It was pretty good, but I think we could use some more. We have a good number of hands-on math resources. We could always use more, but we're in pretty good shape as far as math materials. One big problem, though, is the quality of our math program that we purchased a few years ago. It is simply awful. I can tell you that I, for one, did not want to purchase that program when we decided to back then. It is a major problem, and I would say it is affecting our students' ability to show academic success in math." The principal takes this feedback to heart. He says to himself, "I think that must be the problem. We need to purchase a new math program."

And you guessed it . . . the process starts all over again. I'll bet many of you have experienced this or something very much like it.

Here is the lesson: The program is not the problem. The problem is the location of the program in the "tree." Programs and resources are "in the branches" and are dependent on a good, healthy trunk. The "trunk of the tree" consists of two core systems: unit design and lesson design. Work within these systems must be done first, before initiatives "in the branches" can thrive and produce the outcomes you expect. This will lead to the improved measurable results that your school wants for its students.

Questions for discussion:

1. Core systems work is a key to success in most fields of
   work. Can you think of an example that is outside of
   education?

   _____

   _____

   _____

2. What school–wide efforts have you led or participated
   in that could be categorized as "in the branches"?

   _____

   _____

   _____

3. Thinking back on these efforts, did the results seem to
   fall short of expectations? If so, could it have been a
   "trunk of the tree" issue?

   _____

   _____

   _____

8

Core System #1 - Unit Design

The Measurable Results core systems I'm about to describe are not complicated, flashy, or controversial. The work must be purposeful and intentional, and it requires group effort, collaborative thinking, productive struggle, and time. But in all likelihood, it probably isn't made up of things that aren't familiar to you. Over the course of the rest of the book, pay close attention to each of the pieces of the system, how they are connected, and to the process. All of these elements are extremely important.

The first core system is for unit design (see figure 1.3), and it details the process by which teachers should design units, starting with grade-level standards, followed by creation of learning targets, pacing guides, and then common unit assessments. I recommend that this work begin in reading and math, but it can be done in any subject. Again, not flashy . . . but very effective. We've already talked about learning targets in this book, and I would bet that you have heard of pacing guides and unit assessments. The secret to the power of the unit design process lies not in what you do, but in how you do it. I'll come back to this soon.

Figure 1.3

Core System #1: Unit Design (Standards-Learning Targets-Pacing Guides-Common Unit Assessments)			
Create standards-based learning targets and underpinning targets (UP).	Label each target as a Heavy Hitter (HH) or Secondary (S) target.	Create a pacing guide listing all targets to be taught in each unit, labeled as HH, S, or UP, and with a general time frame in which each unit will be taught.	Create common assessments with each question tied and congruent to a Heavy Hitter target from the unit.

Why should you do unit design work with your staff? Well, besides establishing a strong "trunk" so that your work "in the branches" becomes effective and sustainable, there are a couple of other reasons why this work is so valuable. First, it is based on the premise that students deserve a viable curriculum that guarantees daily instruction in every classroom that is laser-focused on grade-level standards. These are often state standards, but they could also be ACT/SAT standards or whatever set of standards in which you wish to see improved measurable results.

Teachers come to the classroom with wonderful, distinct talents. This is a gift to our students and should be honored with some freedom for lesson design. With that said, resources and instruction that are congruent to standards should not be left to chance. This should be guaranteed in every classroom.

I have a unique perspective when it comes to the notion of a viable curriculum for every child in every classroom. Being the parent of triplets, I always view the concept through that lens. My kids were often in classes together, which means I had three different students bringing home the same graded tests. Also, they were all generally good students, so if two came home with a good grade and one came home with a poor grade, I'd know that one of them didn't study enough. However, if all three came home with a poor grade, I might question whether the teacher had done a thorough enough job teaching the material. Now, most parents don't have the luxury of knowing other kids' grades on tests, so they really have no way of knowing whether their child had not put in the necessary time and effort to perform well on the test or if the teacher had not presented the material in a way that students could understand it.

So what does this mean for creating a viable curriculum for every child? Well, if the unit of study is created so that it is congruent to the standard, starting with learning targets, and then checked by a school administrator, the likelihood of a teacher underperforming or veering way off course is low. What if all my kids have a different teacher? Well, if unit design has occurred as described above, I can at least be sure the material covered and the unit assessments will be the same. This uniformity and accountability can have a huge positive impact on your school by ensuring that teachers aren't going to stray too far from the standards. It also builds a foundation for learning, giving students the tools they need to show standards mastery on tests and state assessments. No longer will the luck of the draw determine a student's performance possibilities, hinging on which teacher the student is assigned. Creating a viable curriculum for all students, regardless of teacher assignment, is a guarantee that our students and parents deserve.

Crowdsourcing unit planning might sound restricting to some. But let me put that fear to rest. All teachers have unique gifts and skill sets, and that is a positive distinction. However, their lessons and units should be rooted in common standards, learning targets to drive lessons, pacing guides that allow and encourage them to share great resources, and unit assessments at the end of units of study. The core system for unit design is not constricting. Instead, anchoring classroom lessons and units in these common elements is actually freeing. It allows teachers to infuse their unique personalities and gifts as they teach while guaranteeing a level of focus and quality across all classrooms school-wide.

The second reason unit design work is important is that it *raises the floor* for instruction in the school. We often try to *raise the roof*—meaning we start where we are and aspire to greater heights, or we set our sights on helping our students who are achieving at an average level to perform at an above-average level. *Raising the floor* is an overlooked aspect of school improvement and deserves significant consideration when doing unit design systems work.

Now, don't get me wrong. This work *will* take your high-achieving teachers and students to new heights. But the overlooked and underrated part of this process has more to do with improving student achievement inside the classrooms of your less talented and lower performing teachers—those who are the opposite of your superstar teachers. The reason? In addition to not being as talented and skilled, these teachers are frequently using poorly designed assessments, asking low-level questions, utilizing resources with poor congruence to grade-level standards, and perhaps not even teaching the grade-level standards. They are not just doing a poor job delivering and assessing learning; they are also using ineffective resources.

Measurable Results unit design work is done in collaborative groups of teachers and then quality controlled by school and district administrators. Stronger teachers within the group provide leadership, making certain that the first draft of learning targets are congruent to grade-level standards, pacing guides are logically and purposefully designed, and unit assessments are designed with questions aligned to the standards. Even if your weaker teachers still struggle with lesson delivery, they will at least create lessons using learning targets that are congruent to grade-level standards, utilize standards-aligned resources that were procured by the group, and end the unit with an assessment made up of standards-aligned questions. By making unit design process collaborative and including superstar teachers, mastery and academic success in lower performing teachers' classrooms will improve.

As we get begin outlining the unit design process, it's important to note that both core systems—unit design and lesson design—rely on two concepts: congruence and quality control. As outlined in chapter 4, *congruence* is perfect alignment with the grade-level standard. It applies to the learning targets written from the standard, resources used in the lesson, written and verbal questions, and any resources used to teach the target/standard. Lack of congruence typically comes down to the verb in the standard. You may remember the example from my own classroom of a standard with the verb *justify* that I planned a lesson around. I did everything else correctly, but I never had the students *justify* their answers or reasoning. If the teacher falters in this way, he has taught a seemingly effective lesson that is, in reality, below grade level or (at best) not aligned with the level of the standard. This happens in schools across the country every day, and it has huge, negative implications for measurable academic results.

The second concept, quality control, has a clear connection to congruence. Quality control is part of what makes the unit design process, at least initially, more powerful than the products that are created. When teachers first attempt to write learning targets that are congruent with grade-level standards or create unit assessments with questions that are congruent with learning targets, their first attempt probably will not be high quality. This is challenging work, and it will be new work for many of them. They will not have developed the skill set yet. It is vital that school administrators (preferably in conjunction with district administrators) quality control the teachers' work. Each learning target, pacing guide, and question on every unit assessment will need to be checked for congruence, quality, clarity, comprehensiveness, and rigor. After quality control, administrators should give the teachers feedback and have them make corrections. Doing so hones their skill set, and they benefit from the process. Students benefit, as well. The quality control process produces a version 2.0, 3.0, and so on of the product. Eventually, the product becomes extremely polished and congruent. When this happens, high student achievement in the school will become an unstoppable force.

Let's get into the four steps of Core System #1: Unit Design.

Step 1: Standards to Learning Targets

Based on work by Rick Stiggins and others, Step 1 starts with a simple three-column chart.[3] In the first column, all the grade-level standards to be taught during the year should be placed, one standard in each row. In the middle column, learning targets that represent the standard should be written.

Learning targets should be:

1. Attentive to key wording within the standard. Learning targets should be written in such a way that they do not change the verb, key nouns, or context of the standard. If the verb in the standard is *analyze*, then the verb in the targets should also be *analyze*. Key nouns from the standard, like *conflict* from a reading standard on fiction, or *angle* from a geometry standard, should also be reflected in the targets. If there is a context such as *in a set of numbers* or *in real-world situations*, that context should also be reflected in the targets.

2. Bite-sized. This simply means that a target can be taught in one lesson, with a significant level of student mastery expected. Depending on size and density, you may need to create several learning targets to cover a single standard. Note that there is some autonomy to be exercised by the collaborative group of teachers here. What can be taught in one lesson must be reasonable and rational, but there is often some gray area here, and it is very appropriate to allow teacher discretion. (See figures 1.4 and 1.5.)

Figure 1.4
Math (5th Grade)

Standard	Learning Targets	Underpinning Targets
KY.5.NBT.3 Read, write, and compare decimals to thousandths. a. Read and write decimals to thousandths using base-ten numerals, number names, and expanded form. b. Compare two decimals to thousandths based on the meanings of the digits in each place, using >, =, and < symbols to record the results of comparisons.	1. I can read and write decimals to thousandths using base-ten numerals. 2. I can read and write decimals to thousandths using number names. 3. I can read and write decimals to thousandths using expanded form. 4. I can compare two decimals to thousandths based on meanings of the digits in each place, using >, =, and < symbols to record the results of comparisons.	I can read and write multi-digit whole numbers using base-ten numerals. I can read and write multi-digit whole numbers using number names. I can read and write multi-digit whole numbers using expanded form. I can read and write decimals to thousandths. I can compare numbers using >, =, and < symbols to record the results of comparisons.

Figure 1.5

English / Language Arts (8th Grade)

Standard	Learning Targets	Underpinning Targets
RI 8.3 Analyze how an author uses comparisons, analogies, or categories to make connections among and distinctions between ideas over the course of a text.	1. I can analyze how an author uses comparisons to make connections among and distinctions between ideas over the course of a text. 2. I can analyze how an author uses analogies to make connections among and distinctions between ideas over the course of a text. 3. I can analyze how an author uses categories to make connections among and distinctions between ideas over the course of a text.	I can analyze the interactions between individuals over the course of a text. I can analyze the interactions between events over the course of a text. I can analyze the interactions between ideas over the course of a text. I can analyze how and why individuals develop over the course of a text. I can analyze how and why events develop over the course of a text. I can analyze how and why ideas develop over the course of a text.

The final part of Step 1 includes the completion of the column on the far right. Once again borrowing a term from Rick Stiggins, this column is for targets known as *underpinning targets*.[4] *Underpinning targets* are a safety net or a building block. They are targets from a previous grade-level standard that are necessary in order for the student to master the current learning target. When viewing the newly written targets in the middle column, the collaborative team of teachers may agree that the majority of their students are typically not ready for that particular grade-level standard when they first encounter it. Teachers should have the autonomy to write underpinning targets for use in these situations. Doing so will allow each teacher to have a learning target each day, meet students at their level of mastery, and remain laser-focused on teaching bite-sized chunks of the content. After spending a day on the underpinning target, the teacher can use the on-grade-level target (from the middle column) during the next day's lesson.

Caution: I would resist requests from teachers to write underpinning targets that reflect grade-level material that is more than two years below grade level. While I realize that there are students who are more than two grade levels below their peers, crafting whole-class learning targets that reflect this is counterproductive. As always, teachers should strive to meet students where they are academically and build from there. There is no need to have an endless litany of underpinning targets spanning many grade levels below the one they teach.

One final note about underpinning targets: Teachers should only use underpinning targets when it is absolutely necessary. It is always preferable to create a lesson around the grade-level learning target(s) and "meet students where they are academically" at the beginning of the lesson—even if you have to meet them at a lower level verb and scaffold up to the grade-level verb by the end of the lesson—rather than spending an entire lesson on an underpinning target.

Quality control for administrators: When Step 1 is completed, this is the first opportunity for administrators to check for congruence, quality, comprehensiveness, and rigor. Focusing on the middle column, first check to make sure that the targets written in each cell fully represent each standard. It is important to make sure that all key segments of the standard are reflected in the targets that have been written by the teachers.

As mentioned earlier, I often find that teachers become overwhelmed when looking at the standards and trying to create lessons that reflect them. One way to "couch" Step 1 with teachers is to encourage them to write the learning targets in such a comprehensive way that the teacher does not have to look at the standards anymore. If she can simply teach each of the targets this year to mastery, she will have no need to look at the standards. I have seen this approach result in reduced stress for teachers. The standards are often overwhelming to read, daunting to plan for, and very difficult for administrators to ensure that they have been taught fully. Teaching with learning targets makes planning intentional, manageable, and focused.

The second part of the quality control process is to make sure that each target is congruent to the standard. Checking for congruence during this step is fairly simple—make sure that each target is bite-sized and that it reflects the same verb, key nouns, and context (if applicable) as the standard.

Step 2: Apply Labels to Learning Targets

In Step 2, all of the newly written targets need to be given a label. Those in the far right column have already been named *underpinning targets*, so their label will be UP. In the middle column made up of targets written directly from the standard, two different labels need to be designated. The first label, Heavy Hitters (HH), needs to be applied to 90 percent or more of the targets. Heavy Hitters are just that—targets that have a heavy impact on current and future academic success. You might say that they are the targets that might cause the teacher to "lose sleep" if the students have not mastered them.

The second type of targets to be labeled are the remaining 10 percent or less—Secondary targets (S). It is important to note here that Heavy Hitters are not "power standards," a term we commonly hear in K–12 education. That is, we are not choosing to prioritize targets from certain standards and eliminate others. In every classroom, all HH and S learning targets will be taught and assessed by the year's end. The difference in how we will treat the two target categories relates to assessment, and I will outline that in Step 4.

Step 3: Pacing Guides

Now that all targets have been written, they need to be placed on a pacing guide that denotes how many units of study there will be, names of the units (optional), the targets that will be taught in each unit, and the general time frame within which each unit will be taught (see figure 1.6 below). It is a simple cut-and-paste from the three-column chart in Step 1. Be sure that the target labels remain with each target as it is transferred to the pacing guide.

Figure 1.6

Pacing Guide (5ᵗʰ Grade Math)

Unit 1: Working with Numbers (mid-Aug to first week of Sept)	Unit 2: Name (time frame)
• I can read and write decimals to thousandths using base-ten numerals. (HH) • I can read and write decimals to thousandths using number names. (HH) • I can read and write decimals to thousandths using expanded form. (HH) • I can compare two decimals to thousandths based on meanings of the digits in each place, using >, =, or < symbols to record the results of comparisons. (HH) • LT #5 • LT #6 • LT #7 • LT #8 • LT #9 • LT #10 • I can read and write multi-digit whole numbers using base-ten numerals. (UP) • I can read and write multi-digit whole numbers using number names. (UP) • I can read and write multi-digit whole numbers using expanded form. (UP) • I can read and write decimals to thousandths. (UP) • I can compare numbers using >, =, or < symbols to record the results of comparisons. (UP) • UP #5 • UP #6 • UP #7	• LT #1 • LT #2 • LT #3 • LT #4 • LT #5 • LT #6 • LT #7 • LT #8 • LT #9 • LT #10 • LT #11 • LT #12 • UP #1 • UP #2 • UP #3 • UP #4 • UP #5 • UP #6 • UP #7 • LT #8
Unit 3: Name (time frame)	Unit 4: Name (time frame)
Unit 5: Name (time frame)	Unit 6: Name (time frame)
Unit 7: Name (time frame)	Unit 8: Name (time frame)

Creating a pacing guide seems like such a small step when it comes to measurable academic achievement, but it is actually very important. First, it makes the planning process even more focused and manageable for the teacher. When planning for each day, she can clearly see the bite-sized targets listed for each unit. It is simply a matter of creating at least one lesson per target and assessing student mastery in a congruent way at the end of that lesson. Second, the general time frames for each unit allow teachers who teach the same grade level and subject to share congruent teaching resources, plan collaboratively, and analyze student work. As mentioned earlier, this is a vital piece of the *raising the floor* aspect of the Measurable Results core systems.

There are a few other caveats about the pacing guide that principals need to know:

1. Instead of exact dates, I recommend that teachers assign a general time frame for teaching each unit. For example, the time frame of "mid-August to the first week of September" is better than "August 16–September 6." Due to the nature of teaching, it is inevitable that teachers will get a few days ahead or behind schedule as they teach. This is completely normal, but teachers who are high achievers will experience stress if there are specific

dates listed and they get behind. This stress is counterproductive and unnecessary. A general time frame is sufficient.

2. Teachers may ask if a particular learning target can be placed in multiple units. The answer is yes, but with one clarification. Sometimes, a learning target legitimately needs to be taught in different units due to different contexts. This is completely acceptable. However, it's important to note that in content areas that are very skill-based (like reading, for instance), there will always be skills that a teacher is managing while simultaneously focusing on teaching another skill. For example, reading teachers will ask comprehension questions throughout the entire school year, nearly every time the class reads a passage. This does not mean that the learning target for comprehension needs to be listed in every unit. Teachers should only place the comprehension target in the units in which they will create and utilize daily lessons solely focused on comprehension. In the other units, the skill of comprehension will be managed, meaning the teacher will likely embed some comprehension questions into daily lessons. But the focus in those lessons will be on a different target, so the comprehension target does not

need to be listed as a target to be taught in those units.

3. Underpinning targets must be listed under their corresponding units on the pacing guide, but it is vital that they are labeled "UP." This signifies that they are a safety net, and because they are below-grade-level targets, they may or may not need to be used with a particular class. If it is necessary to use an underpinning target to meet the students where they are academically, then the teacher will use it. If not, the teacher will use the on-grade-level target. As new teachers are hired in future years and given this pacing guide, keeping the UP label on the target ensures that they will see the distinction. Otherwise, they will be likely to think that all the targets—including the underpinning targets—are on grade level. This can lead to below-level instruction inadvertently becoming the norm in these teachers' classrooms.

4. If the school is being driven heavily by a purchased program or textbook, development of pacing guides can be a bit more complicated. Teachers will want to make the pacing guide mirror the chapters or units in the program. Is this okay? Technically, yes—especially if the school is the only school at its grade levels in the

district or all schools have the same program. However, teachers must embrace and accept two truths:

- Although purchased programs list the state standards that are covered in each chapter or unit, the program publishers do not view congruence the way you now do. As a result, each chapter or unit in the program will have *some* resources and questions that are congruent to the learning target(s) the teacher is teaching on a given day. But there will also be resources and questions within the program that are *not* congruent to the targets. Teachers should not waste time using lessons, resources, and questions from the program that are not congruent to the learning targets that your school has written while implementing the Measurable Results system for unit design.
- The school will eventually adopt another program. When this happens, teachers will need to go back to "square one" and re-create both the pacing guide *and* the common unit assessments.

If the district has multiple schools that contain the same grade levels and the different schools use different programs, I strongly advise against creating a pacing guide that specifically mirrors *any* of the programs. The teachers need to create the learning targets together and then have an honest dialogue—absent any bias stemming from a particular program—about the best way for units to be grouped and organized chronologically. This will be a little messy for a short time, but the galvanization and streamlining of the work is worth it.

Step 4: Common Unit Assessments

Some folks have a bad taste in their mouth when the term *common assessment* is used. This could be for a variety of reasons, but it signifies a bad experience at some point—often one where the district office created some "common" assessments that teachers were forced to administer periodically. Although unintended, this type of effort comes across as a punitive measure with little buy-in from the teachers.

In contrast, Step 4 is the culmination of the important work done by the teachers, as well as the quality control by the administration, in Steps 1 through 3. These steps have ensured that all teachers begin in the same place, with congruent learning targets written by the teachers themselves and quality controlled by their administrators. Learning target labels ensure that each teacher is "on the same page" with colleagues about which targets are the most important and which underpinning targets need to be written as "safety nets." Then, the common pacing guide streamlines the work by ensuring that the same targets are being taught at roughly the same time by teachers of common grade levels and subjects. At the conclusion of the unit design process, common unit assessments guarantee that all teachers finish their units of study in the same place by giving the same unit assessment—designed by them, quality controlled by administrators, with questions that are congruent to the targets listed on the pacing guide for the unit.

As teachers begin the process of creating common unit assessments, there are a few important rules regarding their design:

1. *Common unit assessments should be made up of a variety of question types—multiple choice, short answer, extended response, etc. The assessment that will be used to gauge your measurable results will almost certainly contain a variety of question types and styles. Remember that the verb in the learning target will sometimes determine the type of question that can be used to assess.*

2. *Each question on the assessment must be linked and congruent to a learning target assigned to the unit on the pacing guide.*

3. *All Heavy Hitter targets on the pacing guide must be addressed by at least one question (preferably more) on the common unit assessment.*

4. *Only Heavy Hitter (HH) targets are to be addressed by the assessment. What about Secondary (S) targets? Secondary targets are derived directly from the grade-level standards, which means they are important and must be taught. While not allowed to be reflected in questions on the unit assessments, they should be assessed during daily instruction by formative assessments. They may also appear on quizzes or smaller assessments. The purpose of identifying 10 percent or less of the targets as Secondary is simply to pare down the number of targets assessed on each unit assessment in an effort to keep the number of questions on the assessment reasonable.*

And underpinning targets? They also must not be reflected by questions on the common unit assessments because they are below grade level and, over time, the common assessments will become the "bar" to which every teacher aspires. In order to maximize academic success in a sustainable way, the "bar" needs to be an on-grade-level assessment of standards.

Now that the final step in the unit design process is completed (building common unit assessments), the teachers in your building can walk into a PLC with:

- Daily and periodic performance data for each individual student, based on learning target mastery during the most recent unit of study.
- Individual question breakdowns so that the teacher can easily see which questions each student missed, questions that subgroups of the class missed, and questions that the majority of the class missed. This can lead to great conversation about grouping students for reteaching, extension activities for students who excelled, and examination of weak or poorly written questions.
- Specific standards and learning targets that were partially mastered or non-mastered by some or the majority of the class. These are easy to see because each question is linked to a bite-sized learning target.
- Resources that they will use to reteach the targets. These are great to examine together and look for congruence.
- Individual and class averages from each period of the day (if the teacher has multiple classes of the same section or subject), as well as results from other teachers who teach the same course, grade level, or subject.

- Exemplary samples of student work from short answer or extended response questions that teachers can use when modeling during lessons.

With common assessments, there is so much great material to discuss in PLCs. I have watched it happen in my schools. I can't overemphasize the difference in the quality of academic conversations that principals have with their teachers after building common unit assessments. They provide everything needed for the type of data-rich and student-focused conversations that we all want to have with our teachers. If you can couple this with frequent, unannounced walk-through observations (more on that later), the potential for achievement under your leadership grows exponentially.

Quality Control for Administrators: This is your second major opportunity for determining congruence through quality control. Each question on each unit assessment has been linked to a learning target. It is your job to make sure that, if the student gets the question correct, it means he has mastered the entire target. If so, the question and target are congruent. If not, adjustments need to be made.

In addition, you need to be sure that each Heavy Hitter (HH) target on the pacing guide is well-represented and assessed on the unit assessment. Again, all HH targets must be assessed.

We touched on this earlier, but as you progress through unit design with your staff, one of the fascinating realizations is that the *process* is initially much more powerful than the *product*. You will start to see improved, measurable academic results from students almost immediately—even though you likely will not be finished with the Measurable Results systems work for three to four years. As you and your teachers complete the work and create tools to use, you will make revisions each year—resulting in versions 2.0, 3.0, and so on. The process will continue to be powerful, but as time goes on, the products you create and use in classrooms will also become much more polished, congruent, and well-written. Eventually, they will become nearly flawless. When that day comes, the new skills acquired by your staff through the *process*, coupled with exemplary *products* that have been created and are being used in classrooms across your school or district, create a snowball effect on student achievement. Positive momentum will build. This is a recipe for achieving and sustaining the absolute highest levels of success year after year.

My first experience with the Measurable Results core system for unit design was during my time as chief academic officer at the district level. As a principal, I had done some success-criteria / end-of-the-year benchmark work in my schools. But I had never truly worked with my teachers to turn standards into learning targets, categorize them, put them on a pacing guide, and build unit assessments using them. This unit design system had taken years to recognize and then create, so it was new work for my team and me. We made the decision to implement it in all of the schools in our district at once.

My talented instructional coach, Maureen, was my partner as we did the work. She and I were the quality control team. When the teachers created their first versions of the learning targets, pacing guides, and unit assessments and we began to quality control them, the quality was not very good. At first, we were discouraged. But we strongly believed the work we were doing was the right work and would eventually be worth it. We realized that we would have to endure the current school year and probably accept that improvement may not happen that year, so we just committed to getting the quality control work done with the expectation that improved measurable results were going to take a while. Question by question, on every common unit assessment in reading or math at every grade level, we looked for quality, congruence, and rigor. We gave feedback, then met with the teachers and asked them to make the needed improvements and resubmit. As you can imagine, we were not able to stay ahead of every grade level with our quality control. Therefore, some of the teachers actually used version 1.0 of the unit assessments they had built—which, again, were very low quality.

But as the school year progressed, something terrific and unexpected happened. As students began to take benchmark assessments and other diagnostic exams, we saw marked improvement. As we visited classrooms, we noticed that teachers were asking better verbal questions and adhering congruently to the language of the standard. Even though the questions on the unit assessments were not great, the teachers began writing great questions to use at the end of their lessons. You could tell that our quality control feedback had led them to become more knowledgeable about their standards and more intentional about teaching and assessing them daily. It was clear that the process for unit design was more powerful than the initial product. At the end of the year, students across all grade levels K–12 and in all of our schools made noticeable gains on the state assessment.

The first Measurable Results core system—unit design—is a vital step toward long-term student academic success. There is little else that will provide the same return on investment of your time, effort, and focus. You'll see significant improvement, and the work within this process will anchor instruction for years to come.

Questions for discussion:

1. In core systems unit design work, why is the process powerful and how does it lead to improved measurable results right away?

   _____

   _____

   _____

2. Once common assessments are created, how many different ways can you anticipate that you'll be able to use them in professional learning communities (PLCs) and/or with individual teachers?

   _____

   _____

   _____

3. The four unit design steps are like pieces of a puzzle. In your own words, how do they fit together to improve standards mastery, and therefore measurable results?

   _____

   _____

   _____

9

Digging into the Benefits of Unit Design

In both schools where I served as elementary school principal, we were not the only elementary school in the district. As you can imagine, there was some friendly competition among the schools. Like all rivalries, some folks can take the competitive aspect too far. But for the overwhelming majority of the staff, it was friendly. We wanted the students in the other schools to do well—we really did. We just wanted our students to do a little better. Each school operated independently with its own best practices, programs, and strategies that worked best. For my staff members who were a little overzealous about the competition, our way of doing things was top-secret. According to them, we shouldn't share ideas with the other schools, much less collaborate with them on standards work and curriculum design. Doing so would give them the competitive edge and lessen our chances of being the top elementary school in the district. This mindset was problematic for a couple of reasons.

First, we all got into education to help kids and their families realize a better future. When I say "kids," of course, I don't mean only the ones who attend my school; I mean *all* kids. This perspective is important and, as a principal, I had to spend time instilling it in my staff. It became the definition of "friendly competition." As a school, we wanted our students to do a little better than the other schools. There is nothing wrong with that. But it was important that we shared our great ideas and practices with other schools because it would benefit *all* kids. Doing so fits within each of our missions as educators.

Second, many students in our schools were transient. It wasn't unusual for a student to move around to different schools inside the district within the course of just a few weeks or months. This was a major barrier to student academic success. Since our schools all had different pacing guides, different core instructional programs, and an altogether different curriculum, these students were missing huge chunks of content and skills as they moved from our school to the other schools and then back again within the same school year. There was no backup plan. They simply missed content and skill development that they would never get back again. Some of this content served as a foundation for learning in the next grade level or even years down the road. Missing important content in this way put transient students on the road to academic failure through no fault of their own. As a school and as a district, we realized we had to do better.

As I have mentioned previously, one way that districts often try to address this issue is to buy common programs for all of the schools to use. I get the logic, but the concept of teachers driving day-to-day instruction by "implementing a program with fidelity" has some major issues. As previously mentioned, no matter how well-aligned a program claims to be with a particular state's standards, it is not congruent in the way that we would now define congruence. Even if the program creators have written learning targets, they often won't be as congruent as the targets you've now written.

Another drawback to implementing a program with fidelity is that many programs are designed to encourage teachers to take a "gathering" approach, sprinkling in activities and questions that address a smattering of standards on every page rather than ensuring a laser focus on learning targets from standards. As a result, the teacher feels that she has no choice but to teach every page and use every program activity. Using daily lessons created by a company, in the spirit of "implementing with fidelity," wastes valuable instructional time on activities that aren't perfectly congruent with standards. Like all classrooms that don't have a congruence mindset, the underwhelming improvement in measurable results will show the disconnect.

Let me clarify, however, that programs aren't bad. They can be a fantastic primary resource that teachers use as a critical consumer, while teaching daily lessons from units that are driven by learning targets. The Measurable Results core system for unit design helps teachers keep their focus on standards and unlocks potential for higher levels of student learning. When common grade and subject area teachers from multiple schools across a district work together to unpack standards into congruent learning targets, label those targets as HH, S, or UP, organize the targets into a pacing guide, and then create common unit assessments driven by the targets, the effect is positive and multifaceted. The process allows collaboration to skyrocket—teachers can share resources and best practices that have an impact on student success. And believe me, even in schools that compete with each other, the teachers will share. Spending time together doing the work has a bonding effect, so those relationships will lead to more collaboration. Beyond that, it is just the right thing to do. The teachers will recognize that helping each other fits within their mission as educators. Once administrators build the foundation by facilitating this work, the teachers will collectively work to improve at their craft.

The last impact, though, is one of the most important. Remember all of those kids who are transient, moving from your school to other schools in the district and back multiple times during the year? Can you picture those students who miss huge chunks of content and skills that they will never be taught, leading to future failure? Once the unit design work is complete, common grade and subject area teachers will begin teaching the same targets, in the same order, at approximately the same time. If they are using different resources (and even programs) to teach those targets, that is fine. The key is that teachers at School A are teaching each unit at approximately the same time as School B. If a student transfers back and forth multiple times, he just picks up where he left off. This is gap reduction addressed in a proactive, systemic way.

Guaranteeing a viable curriculum for every child is one of the most impactful aspects of the Measurable Results core system for unit design. When schools and districts become laser-focused on teaching grade-level standards in a congruent way, academic results improve. Every child benefits, in every classroom within a school or among all schools in a district. All those kids who began to fail hopelessly once they moved from school to school a few times have a great chance of success now due to some proactive work that we (the adults) did. If we can make that kind of difference for all kids in all schools within our district, we should embrace the opportunity to do so.

Questions for discussion:

1. *Friendly competition among schools is healthy, but keeping great practices a secret is not. Why?*

   _____

   _____

   _____

2. *How can you instill a healthy balance in your staff between friendly competition and sharing great ideas and practices that benefit students?*

   _____

   _____

   _____

3. *How does the core system for unit design create a viable curriculum for every child?*

   _____

   _____

   _____

10

Pacing and Planning for Unit Design Work

When I coach schools and districts on the core system for unit design, they get fired up! They are ready to do the work and want to get started right away. As a quick review, the work consists of four basic steps:

1. Unpack grade-level standards into learning targets (including underpinning targets).
2. Label the learning targets that are directly from the standards as Heavy Hitters or Secondary targets.
3. Create a pacing guide with every learning target placed into at least one unit of study.
4. Create common unit assessments, with every question reflective of and congruent to an HH learning target.

Because unit design work happens best in collaborative groups of teachers from multiple schools, much of it has to happen on teacher development or professional learning days. As a result, it is often planned for the summer. But as I said, districts are fired up and ready to go. They will often ask, "How much can we get done in one day, or two to three days? How long does it take to get the whole process completed the first time?"

The good news is that the first three steps can be completed in two to three days. Writing the learning targets is slow at first. But once teachers get into a rhythm, it starts moving much more quickly.

As a quick reminder, learning targets need to be quality controlled by the school (and district) leadership team soon after they are written to make sure that:

1. Each target is congruent to the standard it comes from, meaning each target aligns with the verb, key nouns, and context from the standard. It's also important to be sure that no unnecessary language has been added.
2. Each group of targets from one standard fully represents the whole standard, meaning no pieces of the standard have been overlooked and are not reflected in a target.
3. Any standards that require underpinning targets have those in place.

After this process is completed, the targets need to be labeled. This does not really take that much time. Ninety percent or more of the targets need to be labeled as Heavy Hitters, so this part of the process really boils down to the question, "Are there any targets that we would consider as Secondary targets, and if so, which ones?"

Creation of the pacing guide can take some time, but the details behind that have been covered in a previous chapter. Teachers should consider:

1. In what order should the targets be taught?
2. How will targets be bundled into units?
3. Will the units be named?
4. How many times will a given target appear in multiple units?
5. If schools have different programs that they use as a core resource, how will the units be built so as not to favor a particular program?
6. What general time frame for teaching will be assigned to each unit?

Again, these three steps can be completed in two to three days. They are foundational and critical to student success. Even with no common unit assessments built, schools will begin to see student success after completing these three steps because of the focus on teaching grade-level standards through learning targets in the order outlined on the pacing guide. Teachers will also now have common learning targets to build daily lessons around. This will have a huge impact right away.

But the step that still needs to be completed is the one that leads to a consistent, continuous upward trajectory of measurable results. It is also the step that is the most challenging and time-consuming. Common unit assessments need to be built. A general time frame for this work to be completed is to build one to two common unit assessments per day.

When teachers and administrators begin this step in the process, they often have some of the same initial questions:

Question: *What makes a question congruent to a learning target?*

Answer: For a question to be congruent to a target, it means that the student has mastered every piece of the learning target if he gets the answer correct. If this is not the case, it means that either the learning target is not "bite-sized" enough and needs to be split into multiple, smaller targets, or the question needs to be written differently.

Question: *Can I use the chapter/unit test from the program I'm using?*

Answer: You can use questions from your program's assessments if they are congruent to the targets your team has written. It is unlikely that every question on a chapter/unit assessment in your program is perfectly congruent to the targets you wrote. Remember, you should not blindly trust that questions or lessons in a program are perfectly aligned to particular standards— even if they say they are.

Question: *Do we have to create our own questions from scratch, or can we use questions we find online or from other resources?*

Answer: You do not have to write your questions from scratch. They just have to be congruent to your targets. You can use questions from online question banks, programs (old or new), or elsewhere. But be careful. It is up to *you* to make changes to questions to make them congruent to the target to which you have assigned the question.

As you and your staff complete the unit design process, it's important for administrators to build in considerable time for quality control. The process will become even stronger if you can include other administrators and superstar teachers on your quality control team. As mentioned before, the first few versions of learning targets, pacing guides, and common assessments will likely need significant edits. This is just the nature of doing the work for the first time. Meticulously writing/curating questions that are perfectly congruent to learning targets is a unique skill that takes time to master. As your teacher teams submit the products they have created, you should check for congruence, give them feedback, and ask them to go back to make improvements. Through the productive struggle that this creates, they will slowly become experts in their standards and in writing congruent, on-grade-level questions, as well. This will have a lasting impact on the success of students in their classrooms, and the school will see an immediate boost in student achievement even though the assessments are not high-quality at first. As I mentioned before, the *process* is initially more powerful than the *product*. The *product* will eventually catch up with the *process*, and an extremely high level of student achievement will become the norm.

Questions for discussion:

1. *Think about your professional development plans for the upcoming semester(s) and summer(s). How can you carve out the maximum amount of time possible for core systems unit design work?*

   _____

   _____

   _____

2. *Many schools use textbooks or programs as the driver of daily instruction. How can you help your teachers make the critical shift to daily lessons driven by learning targets, with textbooks and programs used as a primary resource?*

   _____

   _____

   _____

3. *Quality control work is a key element of all high-performing organizations. Who will you include on your quality control team and how will you keep your expectations consistent?*

   _____

   _____

   _____

11

Core System #2 - Components of an Ideal Lesson

Now we are ready for the second Measurable Results core system—lesson design. I often call it the "components of an ideal lesson" (see figure 1.7). Let's start with the acknowledgment that lesson planning structure can be a sore spot with teachers. There are many factors that come into play when planning tomorrow's lesson. From a teacher's perspective, one might be tempted to say something like:

- Listen, I am a professional. I have my own style and deserve some freedom.
- I am good at some things, and I design my lessons in a way that makes those strengths work for me.

- Every group of students has different needs and every class has a different dynamic. A strategy that works for my third-period class may not work for my sixth-period class.
- Not all content is created equally, so lesson structures cannot be a "one size fits all."
- Don't fence me in or try to stifle me. Trust me. I've got it.

Figure 1.7

Components of an Ideal Lesson

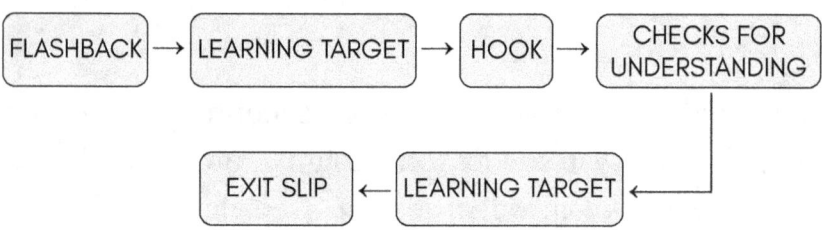

As a teacher, I valued the actionable feedback—both praise and critical guidance—that my principal gave me. I loved that the praise was affirming and the constructive criticism gave me something to work on. I made adjustments, which made my job easier and helped my students learn at high levels. She also led our staff in discussions about what the key parts of effective lessons were. This information helped me as a teacher, so as a brand-new principal, I knew that I wanted to emulate those actions.

As I started observing classrooms, I noticed that we had what I called "pockets of excellence." One classroom would have brilliant instruction happening, the next would be good, the next would be great, and the next would be average or below average. There was no consistency whatsoever in what I was seeing. The excellent classrooms looked nothing like each other, and they did not resemble the good classrooms, either. In fact, there were very few common threads when it came to instructional practices in my building. I had embraced that my primary role as a school leader was to determine who my superstars were and try to make as many of my other teachers look, act, teach, and generally be like my superstars. We were a *long way* from achieving that goal.

I decided to do two things. First, I dedicated myself to learning about my superstar classrooms. I talked to those teachers about what made their students excel, and I both listened and looked for common threads as I learned. Second, I visited high-performing classrooms in other schools in my district and in other districts. In these classrooms, I also talked with superstar teachers about what they were doing that resulted in high-level measurable results. I continued to look for common threads.

In some of the high-performing schools, I noticed something that was very impactful. As I visited classroom after classroom, they didn't have the same "pockets of excellence" that I had. Sure, there were teachers of varying talent and skill levels. But lessons in one classroom *did* resemble lessons in the others. These schools had determined some key components that should be present in all lessons. As you can imagine, the superstar teachers utilized these components at the highest levels, and this allowed the principal to focus on her primary role: scaling the implementation of the lesson components utilized in the superstar classrooms to all classrooms. The basic components were already in place school-wide, so the teachers were using the same terminology and generally "speaking the same language." The principal's job was simply to help all teachers learn to maximize the components of the lesson in a similar way to the superstar teachers.

As you can probably guess, I began to see many of those same components in the superstar teachers' classrooms in my own building. We might have called them by a different name or discovered them a different way, but those best practices existed in my building, just as they did the high-performing schools. The problem was that those components weren't in all of my other classrooms, or they appeared sporadically. I realized that I had to work with my staff to learn about these components and how to use them, get on the same page, provide training, and then commit myself to being in all classrooms often so that I could coach and praise. It became the work that defined my career.

Eventually, we packaged these best practices of lesson design into what has become the second core system—Components of an Ideal Lesson. These are components that should be evident in every lesson in every subject (K–12). This means that no matter if I am in a kindergarten classroom or an Advanced Placement Physics classroom, I should see these elements. While they *can* happen in the order in which I will outline them, this isn't a necessity. The components just need to be present. Once in place, the principal's ability to move the school forward instructionally will become much more manageable. Instilling the Components of an Ideal Lesson into every classroom is work that is both manageable and worth the time you will spend on it.

Component 1: Flashbacks

If you poll a general group of teachers, asking them if they use flashback (or bell ringer) questions during their lessons, many will say yes. However, if you ask them what the purpose of their flashbacks is, they might give a variety of responses:

- "I use them to review what we did in class yesterday."

- "I use them to go over homework questions from the previous night."
- "I use them to review what we've been doing this week, or in the current unit of study."
- "I use them to get the students ready for today's lesson."

None of these are inherently a bad use of class time. When done well, any of those could benefit the academic success of students. If you want to review what's been happening in class, that is okay. However, that is not the purpose of flashbacks within the Components of an Ideal Lesson.

At the core, flashbacks are a spiral review structure. They are not meant for review of recent content. Rather, they are meant to consistently recycle content that was taught in previous units, keeping it fresh on students' minds throughout the year.

Here's how they work:

When students enter the classroom each day, teachers should build two to three flashback questions into their daily classroom routine. The questions must have been purposefully, systematically chosen by the teacher. For instance, Unit 1 may have been taught between September 1 and October 1. The teacher needs to plan for which days or weeks throughout the year that he will administer flashback questions from Unit 1. It could be that Unit 1 flashback questions are given during the second week of November, the first week after Winter Break, the first week of March, and again during the last week of April. As the year progresses and Unit 2 is taught, the teacher will plug in days/weeks in which questions from Unit 2 will be administered.

Teachers have autonomy in scheduling flashback questions throughout the year, but the non-negotiable should be:

1. Flashback questions are administered every day.
2. The questions clearly come from previously administered formative assessment questions in previously taught units.
3. The teacher has a plan schedule that ensures that learning targets from previous units will be addressed in flashbacks multiple times during the school year.

Let's contrast this with traditional teaching methods. In many classrooms, teachers wait until the end of the year or semester to do multi-day, grueling cram sessions to review the content that has been taught during the year. I was certainly guilty of this as a teacher, and the result is not surprising. Either the students don't remember the content, or many of them have to go back to their previous work and essentially relearn what they were taught—and might have even mastered! It is a no-win situation for everyone, and it can be frustrating for both the teacher and the students. It is an indicator that the students have not committed the content and skills to long-term memory, and definitely cannot transfer and utilize them in new situations. In short, they have not learned the standards. Although this practice has been prevalent for decades, we know that it does not work. A lesson design system including daily flashbacks will make a difference.

Here is an added bonus: a daily plan using flashbacks is great for classroom management. Often, student misbehavior can begin right after the class period begins and the students are waiting for the teacher to start the lesson. Maybe he is taking attendance or gathering materials to distribute before the lesson begins. This is totally acceptable, but not always effective. Over the course of the year, students get accustomed to these minutes at the beginning of class being free time. This lack of structure makes the transition to learning time more difficult for both the teacher and the students. On the other hand, if students get used to the routine of entering the classroom every day and immediately beginning their flashbacks, it can significantly curb off-task behavior and start the class period off on a very productive note. Not only that—it also helps ensure that the teacher is instructing bell to bell, and this should be a goal for all classrooms.

Component 2: State the Learning Target(s)

In chapter 7, we took a pretty deep dive into the purpose of learning targets. Remember the discussion on "light bulb" moments, including how we can get addicted to them and start structuring our lessons in such a way as to create them? That is not a great way to learn, so Component 2 says that as soon as flashbacks are completed and the day's lesson is ready to begin, we should state the learning target to/with the class. Rather than *reveal* the lesson's learning intention after the lesson is half over, we should clearly *articulate* what the learning intention is for the day before the lesson begins.

Also, don't forget that learning targets—once they are pulled from the standards in bite-sized chunks and quality controlled for congruence to the standard—become the congruence *lens* through which teachers view the rest of the lesson, including:

- Resources and materials used
- Questions asked during the lesson (written and verbal)
- Questions used on the daily formative assessment

Remember to pay close attention to the target's verb, key nouns, and context (if applicable). While the lesson does not have to begin at the level of the verb in the target, the students *do* need to be able to perform at the level of the verb by the end of the lesson.

Component 3: Hook

Before I learn something new, it always seems best if I have an idea of what I am about to learn (see Component 2), but it also helps if my curiosity is piqued and/or if the new information can be connected to my previous knowledge. Component 3 addresses these needs. In each lesson, the teacher needs to have a small window of time in which he *hooks* the class—getting them interested and ready to learn.

A good hook could be a video clip, a story, an image, or an object that students can hold in their hands. I am reminded of a hook that my fourth-grade teacher used nearly forty years ago. We were in science class, learning about the different types of rocks. My teacher had been on an anniversary trip to Hawaii and brought back some igneous (volcanic) rocks. I attended a small, very rural school in a farming community, and my particular grade level was one of the smallest in the school. Over the years, we had anywhere from twelve to eighteen students in my class. Suffice it to say that not many of us had ever gotten to see and touch a volcanic rock! Even all these years later, I can recall the rocks being passed around from student to student. I can even feel the weight and texture in my hands. Talk about a great hook! The whole experience probably lasted two or three minutes, and I can remember it vividly all these years later. An effective hook does not have to be elaborate or expensive. It just needs to connect students with the learning that is about to occur.

There is one last tip I will share about effective hooks. When I think of a hook, I think of a common experience shared by all students in the class. With the volcanic rocks, we all held the rocks, and none of us had been to Hawaii or anywhere else to see such rocks. Holding them and hearing about my teacher's anniversary trip, including where she found the rocks, put all of the students on a common level of readiness to learn. This is so important, because the students in our classrooms come from such varied backgrounds and experiences. If we can level the playing field and ensure that all students are ready to learn together, we should.

This component always makes me think about field trips. When teachers plan field trips that are connected to learning, we nearly always teach the unit of study and *then* go on the field trip as a cumulative activity.

Why don't we go on the field trip *before* we teach the unit? Think about the effect that this could have on learning—creating a common experience for all students. If the experience is truly tied to the learning targets that will be taught during the unit, it opens up a world of possibility when it comes to creating lesson hooks. Think of the learning advantage this will give to the students as teachers get them ready to learn today's target by connecting to something that was seen or happened during the field trip. It's a slight adjustment that can have massive learning implications.

Components 4 and 5: Teach New Content: Check for Understanding and Actively Engage Students

Components 4 and 5 are separate in terms of what they represent in the lesson, but I have listed them together because they are a package deal. They are the core of the lesson and consume the largest portion of the class period. They are also the components in which instruction on the learning target is delivered/facilitated by the teacher.

Obviously, Component 4 is laser-focused on the day's learning target. As a teacher, how am I going to meet students where they are academically and get them to demonstrate mastery of the target by the end of today's lesson? This component is one in which the teacher's individual gifts, talents, and abilities can really shine. It is important for each teacher to strictly adhere to congruence in this segment, being mindful and purposeful about the resources and lessons used, as well as the questions asked (verbal and written) as she teaches the day's target. But having said that, two teachers who teach the same target may have lessons that look very different—crafted to each teacher's style, talent, skill, and ability. This is not only acceptable . . . it is a beautiful aspect of the Components of an Ideal Lesson system.

There is, however, one *extremely* important rule within Component 4, and it creates a direct link to Component 5. As the target is being taught, the teacher must adhere to this rule:

While teaching the day's learning target, teachers may only lecture—meaning students are passively listening to the teacher—for one minute per year of age of the students.

This rule, rooted in brain research, comes in many forms from education experts like Mike Rutherford in

The Artisan Teacher,[5] Grace Dearborn of Conscious Teaching, and others.[6] In a nutshell, we can only passively listen and learn for a limited amount of time. As educators, we overestimate how long our students can *actively* learn while *passively* listening. It's a much shorter duration than we would like to think. When students have been passively listening for approximately the number of minutes that equals their age, they reach a saturation point. For those of us who have been in the classroom, it is that moment when the students' eyes glaze over. Suddenly, you realize that while they may still be looking in your direction, they are not hearing you and they definitely are not going to be able to apply what you are teaching. We have all been there. This rule is to help teachers avoid that moment and the lost learning time that comes with it.

So, what happens when the teacher stops lecturing? Enter Component 5. He needs to check for understanding and actively engage the students. Think about it from the teacher's perspective . . . you have just taught a chunk of the learning target for the day. It is time to check for understanding anyway. You might use a cooperative learning structure, a performance task, or a group discussion. You might ask students to solve a related problem or fill out a graphic organizer. As you check for understanding, you will gather some formative assessment data about the class that you can use while teaching the next chunk of the learning target. This is huge. If you can do so while actively engaging the students, their brains will re-engage, and they will enter the next segment of learning with renewed energy and interest.

There is really only one rule related to Component 5: something *different* must happen besides the students passively listening to the teacher. Once he has checked for understanding and actively engaged the students, the students are ready to be taught another chunk of the learning target. After one minute per year of age, the teacher needs to stop, check for understanding, and actively engage the students again. This "toggling" between Components 4 and 5 continues until the day's learning target has been taught and the teacher is ready to assess the students' mastery.

Component 6: Restate the Learning Target

In Component 2, we discussed the importance of the teacher referencing the learning target at the beginning of the lesson. This prepares the students for the learning that is about to occur, which is so much better than hoping for "light bulb moments."

Component 6 follows a very similar rationale. Each day's learning is no mystery. Once the new content has been taught and understanding has been checked, it is time to restate what students have just learned. It may sound trite and meaningless, but it brings closure to the time that has been spent. Restate, or have one or more of the students restate, the day's learning target. Then, move on to assessment.

Component 7: Formative Assessment (Exit Slip)

They say "what is measured gets done." This is so true, but I will expand on this idea. When you measure specifically, you not only make sure that things "get done;" you are producing purposeful, actionable information to help you take the next steps.

When it comes to formative assessment, educators are sometimes all over the place. If I surveyed a general group of teachers and administrators about formative assessment, they would tell me that it can be many things.

- Ask a question and let one student answer? Yes, that's formative assessment.
- Assign small group work and circulate to eavesdrop on the conversations happening in each group? Yes, that's formative assessment.

- Hand out marker boards and pose a question to the class. Then, ask them to show their boards all at the same time, allowing for a general idea of the class's mastery of the question? Yes, that's formative assessment.

These are good strategies, and when used correctly, can be helpful teacher tools. But none of these are the formative assessment that is called for in Component 7. Formative assessment—which I call an exit slip in the Components of an Ideal Lesson— has one major purpose and many ancillary benefits. We administer a formative assessment at the end of every lesson because we need to assess mastery of today's learning target for *every student in the class, every day.*

This step is crucial to achieving measurable results because the teacher has already shown a laser-focus on the day's learning by using a congruent learning target *and* strict adherence to congruence by making sure she has asked questions and used resources that are congruent to that target. Now the lesson just needs to end congruently.

I mentioned earlier that I call formative assessments at the end of a lesson "exit slips." Many people call them other names, like exit tickets or tickets out the door. It really does not matter what you call it. It is simply vital that there is one. It does not have to be complicated either. Below are some best practices for exit slips.

Exit slips:

- Should be three to five questions long, with all questions congruent to the day's learning target. This means if the student answers a question correctly, he/she has mastered the entire learning target that the question is designed to assess. Again, the verb from the target is key.
- Should be made up of a variety of question types—multiple choice, short answer, extended response, graphic organizer (like a Venn diagram or double bubble thinking map for a compare/ contrast target), graph, chart, etc. Just be mindful of one thing: if the teacher desires improved measurable results on a particular assessment, the students need practice showing evidence of mastery answering questions that are designed and formatted like those on that assessment. This is not "teaching to the test," nor is it an attempt to teach "tips, tricks, and cheat codes." Exposing students to questions that are written in a similar way to a particular assessment simply allows the students to show

what they know when they take that assessment. I would argue that it is unfair for students to not have seen a particular type of question all year before taking the test.

When a teacher has the Components of an Ideal Lesson in place daily, it creates a powerful climate for learning. But it does more than that. If I am a student who struggles academically, it may be likely that I have mastered the ability to hide in plain sight. Without the accountability that the components guarantee, I can probably make it out of the classroom on a given day without the teacher knowing that I do not understand the content that was covered during the lesson. This is dangerous because brain research tells us that the time between the end of class today and the beginning of class tomorrow is time in which my brain is processing concepts and information and preparing them for use in short- and long-term memory. If I have a misconception or misunderstanding, that is what my brain is processing and preparing to use in real-life situations. By the time I come back to class tomorrow, those misunderstandings are far more embedded into my learning than they were today. It will be much more time intensive for me to unlearn the incorrect content and concepts and replace them with accurate understanding.

If my teacher is using learning targets to drive the lesson and assessing daily with a congruent exit slip, he knows exactly which students mastered, partially mastered, and did not master today's bite-sized chunk of content. Once he has that specific information, he can do something proactive to make sure that my learning is complete. When this happens, day after day, in lesson after lesson, it becomes a systematic way of teaching. And I, as the struggling student, realize that I can no longer hide. If I am struggling on a given day, my teacher will know it and he will do something about it to help me master what I need to learn. That's powerful because it creates *hope*.

Components of an Ideal Lesson is not a structure designed to make all teachers look like exact replicas of other teachers. Instead, it is a framework of best practice lesson anchors that, when in place, actually free the teacher to embed individual talents in a manner that impacts students in a much more powerful way than lessons designed based on talent alone. When it comes to student achievement, it is a framework that guarantees a laser-focused effort toward student mastery of standards. Improved measurable results will follow.

Questions for discussion:

1. Can you think of instances in which consistent, specific feedback helped you or someone else improve? What made the feedback so helpful?

_____

_____

_____

2. If you observed all of the classrooms in your school today, are there any best practice anchors already in place?

_____

_____

_____

3. Which components of an ideal lesson do you think will have the most immediate impact on student mastery of standards and measurable results in your school?

_____

_____

_____

12

Intervention

As schools implement the Measurable Results core systems, there are developmental levels and a progression that are commonly experienced by both schools and individual teachers. They will inevitably have some of the same questions and barriers. As teachers begin to view their work through a different lens, they realize there are next steps they must take. One such example involves reteaching and intervention.

Before we dive in, let's recap the information you now have at your fingertips. With the core systems in place, teachers have learning targets driving every lesson and every unit. Congruence to the targets influences resources used, and every lesson ends with a formative assessment, or exit slip, that contains three to five questions that are perfectly congruent to the learning target(s) driving the day's lesson. As mentioned before, this exit slip should not come from the homework assignment. It also should not be created using questions from the checks for understanding portion of the Components of an Ideal Lesson. The exit slip is a stand-alone assessment, given daily to every student to assess mastery of the day's target(s).

This brings us to intervention. Once teachers start getting daily, learning-target-based data from exit slips, they now know—without question—which students mastered, partially mastered, or did not master the day's learning target(s) before (or very soon after) the students leave the room. This is powerful. There is no guesswork at this point. As the teacher, I do not have to wait until tomorrow to check the students' homework and assess understanding. I know which students have limited or no understanding of each day's content. With such critically important information, I should feel compelled to provide additional support for these students.

Talking about intervention makes me think about a structure that has been around for many years now—Response to Intervention, or RTI. If you are not familiar with it, RTI groups instructional services to students into three tiers. One of the biggest misconceptions I've seen with RTI is schools not incorporating reteaching into Tier 1.

1. Tier 1—The core curriculum, instruction, and supports that all students receive. This includes regular reteaching by the classroom teacher.
2. Tier 2—Additional time for instruction and supports for students who still struggle even though they are receiving Tier 1
3. Tier 3—More instructional time and supports for students who still struggle even though they are receiving both Tier 1 and Tier 2

Taking a deep dive into tiers of intervention is another book for another day, but I would be remiss if I did not address some key concepts about these tiers as they relate to our Measurable Results core systems. First, before any student is labeled as needing Tier 2 intervention, Tier 1 must be robust, rigorous, congruent with standards, and rooted in best practices. The core systems, as well as other mindsets and best practices that we have explored in this book are all elements of Tier 1.

In order to fully maximize the benefits of Tier 1 for all students, every teacher in every classroom must have a guaranteed, scheduled time at least once per week to provide reteaching to students who partially mastered or did not master the learning targets during the week. It is essential that this time is scheduled and guaranteed to happen. Students who struggle will count on the fact that they get at least one more chance during the week to master the learning targets and be ready to move forward with the rest of the class on Monday. This final piece of Tier 1 is crucial to the Measurable Results system and critical to the academic success of all students.

Here's how it works: armed with daily congruent exit slips, teachers can easily identify which students mastered, partially mastered, or did not master each day's learning target(s), thus providing the valuable information needed for reteaching. In my experience, I have seen reteaching time structured in different ways. Sometimes, a teacher will set aside time on Friday for reteaching Monday's, Tuesday's, Wednesday's, and Thursday's targets. In this model, Friday's schedule will look different than the other days of the week. Students who mastered all the targets for the week will be given real-life application and extension work while the teacher reteaches small groups of students who partially mastered or didn't master the targets.

In other classrooms, teachers may build in daily reteaching time by ending the instructional part of the class period ten to fifteen minutes early. They administer the exit slip, look at the results, and provide reteaching instruction to students immediately. This can be a very effective model, especially in schools with class periods lasting sixty minutes or more. There are many other models, such as reteaching on Wednesdays because the school's master schedule for that day is unique, or on Mondays because it helps the students begin the week by shoring up misconceptions before a new week of learning begins. There is not really a wrong way to do this. The important thing is that reteaching is scheduled during class time, students know it, and it always happens.

In one of my elementary schools, the principal and instructional coach created a regular Friday PLC meeting with teachers called "Bulldog Blueprint" day. It aligned with the Measurable Results core systems, so exit slip data, common assessments, learning targets, and congruence were regular topics. This meeting structure led to intentional reteaching in every classroom, every week, based on data from exit slips. It set the principal and instructional coach up for success, due to the deep, quality conversations it spurred with teachers. In turn, it set the teachers up for success by requiring them to implement the Measurable Results core systems in order to participate in the conversations. The teachers submitted their learning targets and student exit slip data from the week, and the duration of the "Blueprint" meeting was spent building a plan for addressing the reteaching needs of the students. It placed the right people in the room together, with the right data, at the right time. It's a recipe for success.

It should be noted that when teachers first hear about the requirement that they set aside time for reteaching each week, they often become concerned that dedicating a day per week will hinder their ability to cover all of the standards for the year. This is an understandable concern. However, I have seen it implemented in many different schools (elementary, middle, and high), and I have never seen this concern become a reality. In contrast, most teachers tell me they are surprised that they cover all of the standards more quickly than usual.

Let's talk, then, about how a teacher should plan reteaching sessions. The teacher already taught the learning target(s) earlier in the week and it's likely she taught it the best way she knew how. So how does she reteach it? First, let's talk about how *not* to reteach it. As educators, we've all heard the criticism that it is not effective to do the same thing you did the first time— only louder and slower. If the approach did not work the first time, it likely will not work the second time.

When it comes to reteaching based on previously taught learning targets, it is important to remember that there are two kinds of students who need this support. First, there are students who partially mastered the target(s). These students know some of the content and have acquired some of the desired skills. They likely have some common misconceptions. For these students, the teacher should analyze their exit slips by closely examining the questions they missed. This will allow the teacher to uncover the sources of the confusion and focus the reteaching lesson on correcting them.

The second group of students are those who showed non-mastery of the target(s). These students have misconceptions, but they also may be missing core, foundational content and skills from previous grade levels. During reteaching lessons, the teacher should focus on meeting these students where they are academically—building the foundational skills needed and then scaffolding to enable them to access the on-grade-level targets. With the Measurable Results core systems in place, coupled with weekly, guaranteed reteaching, Tier 1 is being addressed in each classroom throughout the school. Many students will thrive with this type of focus, intentionality, and support.

This brings us to Tier 2, which consists of extra, additional instruction and support for students who struggle even though they are receiving Tier 1 instruction. The most dangerous misstep here is identifying a student for Tier 2 intervention without a strong Tier 1 system in place. Before identifying a student as Tier 2, make sure that:

1. The school has done (or, at the least, is in the process of doing) the Measurable Results core systems work.
2. Every teacher, in every classroom, has guaranteed, weekly reteaching in place based on the current week's learning targets (as described in this chapter).

If either or both of these processes are not in place, it is possible that the student is not benefiting from strong enough Tier 1 instruction and support, and therefore may be labeled incorrectly as needing Tier 2 intervention. If both of these are in place and a student is still struggling, the student should be provided Tier 2 services. Tier 2 intervention is pulling a student from the class for additional subject instruction outside of class time (Tier 1). Please note that Tier 2 intervention also works best when it is aligned with current learning targets. For instance, a student who has not mastered basic multiplication shouldn't continually work on that if the class is studying properties of operations or place value. The intervention teacher should work closely with the classroom teacher to provide intervention that is foundational to the lessons being taught daily in the classroom.

If a student still struggles after Tier 1 and Tier 2, as I've described them, then he likely needs Tier 3 intervention. These students often are learning below grade level or even several grade levels. Programming within Tier 3 can include intensive instruction focused on prerequisite skills from several grades below the student's current level. The number of students who require Tier 3 services should be very small once the Measurable Results core systems are being used school-wide.

With powerful, daily data to support intervention and structures to provide weekly reteaching, the unit and lesson design work the school has done will truly flourish. Measurable academic results will soar to new heights and will consistently, continually grow. This type of success is a win-win for all. It benefits students, families, the school, the district, and, over time, the community as a whole.

Questions for discussion:

1. How are the Components of an Ideal Lesson, including exit slips, the starting point for reteaching and intervention?

   _____

   _____

   _____

2. Have you seen standards-based reteaching models that were effective? If so, how were they designed and implemented?

   _____

   _____

   _____

3. What are the differences in approach between reteaching students who showed partial mastery of a target versus non-mastery of a target?

   _____

   _____

   _____

Conclusion

Measurable Results work is powerful. When schools fully commit to implementation of the core systems, I've seen proficiency rates increase by more than 20 percent and novice percentages shrink to less than 10 percent. In high schools that test every student, I've witnessed school-wide ACT composite averages improve by more than three points. Schools that utilize quarterly, nationally normed benchmark assessments that measure academic growth often experience a mean of 1.5 years of student academic growth during a single school year.

This isn't change that flies under the radar—it is dramatic and noticeable. When a school improves in such a vibrant, visible way, it can have a long-lasting impact—changing the perspective of community members, lawmakers, families, and others. But most importantly, this work changes the life trajectory of individual students, opening opportunities that may have never been available without the academic experience they will have in your school.

Measurable Results system implementation isn't a complicated process. It requires patience, persistence, focus, and the willingness to stick with it. It isn't flashy, gimmicky, or something that is outside what should already be happening in all classrooms. In many schools, the elements described in this book are already evident in some classrooms. But far too few. It's the principal's job to change this.

Getting started, it's important to remember the primary role of the principal—to *recognize who the superstar teachers are and make as many non-superstar teachers look, act, behave, and generally be like those superstars.* This rule of school leadership is vital for academic success. Once the superstars have been identified, it's important to spend time in their classrooms, observing them teaching and talking with them. Both the principal and the superstar teachers need to be cognizant of what practices set them apart from the norm. These will eventually become agreements or guarantees adopted by the whole school. At this point, the principal's job is simple. You must keep a laser focus on scaling these practices to every classroom in the school.

The Measurable Results core systems for unit and lesson design give you a head start. They are the scalable best practices and mindsets that are seen in many, many superstar classrooms, like:

- Congruence—classrooms that are driven by congruence showcase lessons that are laser focused on grade-level standards, with resources and questions that are perfectly aligned with the standards. Teachers with a congruence mindset hold the students to mastery of grade-level standards, and it makes a huge difference in the academic success of their students.
- We Control Our Destiny—this mindset permeates high-performing schools. They believe that everything needed to excel academically exists within the walls of the school.
- Trunk of the Tree—schools who spend time and effort implementing the Measurable Results core systems build a foundation, or a healthy *trunk*, that allows for all academic efforts to thrive, including those that might be found *up in the branches*.
- Core System #1: Unit Design—a four-step process that walks collaborative teams of teachers through the process of:

- Pulling comprehensive sets of bite-sized learning targets from the grade-level standards
- Labeling those targets as Heavy Hitter (HH), Secondary (S), or underpinning (UP)
- Strategically organizing the targets into a unit-based pacing guide
- Creating unit assessments that measure mastery of the targets with an emphasis on congruence

- Core System #2: Components of an Ideal Lesson—a lesson structure that:

  - Begins with a learning target or two that drives each lesson
  - Contains seven components that should be included every day, in every lesson, classroom, and subject in grades K–12

- Reteaching—armed each day with powerful, learning-target-based formative assessment data on every student, every classroom teacher must embrace a scheduled time for purposeful reteaching at least once per week.

In a school with empowered superstar teachers and a focused principal who implements the Measurable Results system, academic success rates will improve.

But it's much more than that. The academic experience for every student will improve, and that's a positive for your students and your school. The *process* is initially more powerful than the *products* created, so you'll start to see success very quickly.

Working in the field of education is a calling. It is a service-driven field that puts others and their well-being first. It can lead to a purpose-driven life steeped in positivity and prosperity for ourselves and those around us.

I often say that the field of education is the only one I can think of in which an entire community can be transformed over the course of one generation. Sure, there are many other important jobs in a community, and I do not want to discount them. But when a school positively impacts the life of a student, it also affects the student's current and future families. It might open access to a career field that otherwise would not have been possible for the student, scholarships or apprenticeships that might not have been awarded, and a legacy of educational and professional attainment that the student will instill in his own children. If the school and district have this effect on the lives of many students, their current and future families, and their ultimate trajectory of success experienced by all, this impact shapes a community over time. What other profession can say that it has this potential?

With this type of power and possibility, we must hold ourselves and our students to the highest standard. It is just too important not to do so. If your school is in need of academic improvement, investing in the core systems work described within this book can make all the difference. It leads to an invigorating educational experience for students who graduate having mastered the content and skills within the standards for every grade level. If you could go back and guarantee this result for all students who have been in your classroom and/or school over the years, wouldn't you? Let's improve our practices, enhance the learning experience for our students, and celebrate the measurable results that follow!

About the Author

David Young is a former elementary school teacher, principal, and assistant superintendent – chief academic officer. He now serves as the chief executive officer of the Central Kentucky Educational Cooperative in Lexington, Kentucky. During David's time as a principal, he led two schools to become high performers in Kentucky. As assistant superintendent for ten years of Boyle County Schools in central Kentucky, David contributed to the district's climb from the fiftieth ranked school district in Kentucky (of 175) to the fourth ranked district overall, the number one ranked county school district, and a perennial top five district. At the Central Kentucky Educational Cooperative, David and his staff are using the Measurable Results system to improve the rates of student academic success within all of the cooperative's thirty-two school districts. David resides in Danville, Kentucky, with Holly, his wife of twenty-one years, and their triplets—Mason, Connor, and Emma.

WORKS CITED

1. Whitaker, Todd. *What Great Principals Do Differently*. 2nd ed. Eye On Education, 2011.

2. The New Teacher Project. "The Opportunity Myth." The New Teacher Project, September 25, 2018, www.opportunitymyth.tntp.org. Accessed November 25, 2023.

3. Stiggins, Rick; Arter, Judith; Chappuis, Jan; Chappuis, Steve. *Classroom Assessment for Student Learning: Doing It Right—Using It Well*. 1st ed. Pearson, 2009.

4. Stiggins, Rick; Arter, Judith; Chappuis, Jan; Chappuis, Steve. *Classroom Assessment for Student Learning: Doing It Right—Using It Well*. 1st ed. Pearson, 2009.

5. Rutherford, Mike. *The Artisan Teacher*. Rutherford Learning Group, 2013.

6. Dearborn, Grace. "Rebels with Applause: Brain-Compatible Approaches for Motivating Reluctant Learners." Conscious Teaching, 2013. Web. Accessed January 2, 2014.